CAMBRIDGE

EMPOWER

SECOND EDITION

WORKBOOK
WITH ANSWERS

B1

PRE-INTERMEDIATE

Peter Anderson

CONTENTS

1A DO YOU PLAY ANY SPORTS?

1 VOCABULARY Common adjectives

a Underline the correct words to complete the sentences.

1 The new building opposite the university is *rude* / *ugly* / *all right*. I hate it!
2 Our new teacher is always very *serious* / *silly* / *rude*. We work very hard in her lessons, and she never smiles or laughs.
3 The cakes in the new bakery are *silly* / *serious* / *delicious*!
4 My brother's new girlfriend is *ugly* / *beautiful* / *delicious*. I think she's a model.
5 We played a lot of *silly* / *horrible* / *perfect* games at Sarah's birthday party. I have some really funny photos on Facebook.
6 Lily's a *perfect* / *strange* / *lovely* person. Her grandchildren love visiting her.

b Complete the sentences with the adjectives in the box.

~~boring~~	all right	awful	amazing
delicious	rude	strange	perfect

1 I'm not interested in football. It's so boring.
2 Thanks for the chocolates. They were ________!
3 Look at this beautiful weather – it's a ________ day to go to the beach.
4 The film we watched last night was really ________. I didn't understand it at all.
5 **A** How was the restaurant?
B Oh, it was ________. There are better Italian restaurants in my town.
6 The weather in Scotland was ________. It rained every day.
7 The band were ________! It was the best concert I've ever been to.
8 The waiter at the hotel was ________. He said he couldn't help us because we're vegetarian.

2 GRAMMAR Question forms

a Underline the correct words to complete the questions.

1 How many children *he does have* / *does he have* / *does have he*?
2 Where *did you meet* / *did meet you* / *you met* your husband?
3 *Did he grow up* / *He grew up* / *He did grow up* in this area?
4 What *was like the film* / *was the film like* / *the film was like*?
5 How much *paid you* / *you did pay* / *did you pay* for your smartphone?
6 *Why she go* / *Why she went* / *Why did she go* to the USA?
7 How many films *he made* / *did he make* / *did make he* last year?
8 How *was your holiday* / *your holiday was* / *did your holiday be*?

b Put the words in the correct order to make questions.

1 you / Sarah's friend / are ?
Are you Sarah's friend?
2 work / a bank / he / does / in ?
____
3 you / last month / to New York / go / did / why ?
____
4 like / that new Brazilian / what / restaurant / is ?
____
5 with your sister / who / that man / was ?
____
6 TV programmes / you / do / watch / what type of ?
____
7 go to / did / which university / you ?
____
8 did / how much / cost / the tickets ?
____

1B I'M REALLY INTO SOCIAL MEDIA

1 VOCABULARY Adverbs

a Put the words in brackets in the correct place in each sentence.

1 They see their grandchildren now that they live in Australia. (hardly ever)
They hardly ever see their grandchildren now that they live in Australia.

2 I enjoy watching old Hollywood films. (particularly)
____

3 She hates it when people are late for meetings. (absolutely)
____

4 We go to Italian restaurants, but sometimes we go to Turkish ones. (usually)
____

5 We're sure his flight arrives at Terminal 2, but I need to check. (pretty)
____

6 I hope he brings his beautiful sister to the party! (really)
____

b Underline the correct adverbs to complete the sentences.

1 I love rock music, but I *absolutely* / *especially* / *fairly* like the Foo Fighters. They're my favourite band.
2 He *hardly ever* / *never* / *especially* calls his mother – maybe once or twice a month.
3 I *rarely* / *pretty* / *usually* enjoy horror films, but this one was awful!
4 She's *fairly* / *absolutely* / *rarely* good-looking, but I don't think she's beautiful.
5 I *never* / *absolutely* / *hardly ever* hate maths. I just don't understand it!
6 She *usually* / *particularly* / *rarely* takes her family out for dinner – only when it's her birthday.
7 They love all sports, but they're *fairly* / *really* / *pretty* interested in football. They watch all the matches on TV.
8 It's *pretty* / *usually* / *rarely* cold today, so why don't you take your gloves?

2 PRONUNCIATION Long and short vowels

a 01.01 Listen to the words. Do the letters in **bold** make long or short vowel sounds? Tick (✓) the words with long vowel sounds.

1 ✓ b**ir**thday	6 ☐ s**i**lly
2 ☐ b**a**nk	7 ☐ m**u**sic
3 ☐ cinem**a**	8 ☐ sp**or**t
4 ☐ f**oo**d	9 ☐ fr**ie**ndly
5 ☐ p**ar**ty	10 ☐ bl**o**g

3 GRAMMAR Present simple and present continuous

a Underline the correct verb forms to complete the sentences.

1 She *is loving* / *loves* / *love* reading fashion magazines at the hairdresser's.
2 We usually *are going* / *goes* / *go* to the café opposite the hotel.
3 I *read* / *'m reading* / *reading* a great book in English at the moment.
4 He *does want* / *'s wanting* / *wants* to call his family in Tokyo. Can he use the wi-fi?
5 Why *are you waiting* / *do you wait* / *you waiting* for the bus? Let's walk home.
6 I hardly ever *am visiting* / *visit* / *visits* my cousins in Ireland.
7 She *studies* / *studying* / *'s studying* French politics at university this term.
8 Yes, they're here. They *play* / *'re playing* / *playing* a video game in the living room.

b Complete the conversation with the present simple or present continuous forms of the verbs in brackets. Use contractions where possible.

MEGAN What 1 's Andrea doing (Andrea, do) in that shop?
NAOMI She 2 ________ (buy) some postcards to send to her family.
MEGAN Really? I 3 ________ usually 4 ________ (not send) postcards. I usually 5 ________ (write) a message on Facebook. And sometimes I 6 ________ (post) a few photos of my holiday on Instagram.
NAOMI Yes, me too, but Andrea's grandparents 7 ________ (not use) social media, so she 8 ________ (send) them postcards instead.
MEGAN Oh, and what 9 ________ (Marco and Jack, do) this morning?
NAOMI They 10 ________ (spend) the day at the beach.
MEGAN But Marco 11 ________ (not like) swimming in the sea. He says the water's too cold.
NAOMI Yes, but it 12 ________ (be) really hot today!

c 01.02 Listen and check.

1C EVERYDAY ENGLISH

It was really nice to meet you

1 USEFUL LANGUAGE

Greeting people; Ending conversations

a Underline the correct words to complete the conversation.

SAM Hi, James! [1]*Much / Long / Very* time no see! How are you?
JAMES Hi, Sam. I'm fine, thanks. [2]*What a / What / How* lovely surprise! Great to see you!
SAM Yes, it's really nice [3]*see you / to see you / you see*, too.
JAMES Where are you living [4]*today / this day / these days*?
SAM Oh, not [5]*far from / far of / far away* here. In Park Road, near the sports centre.
JAMES Oh, [6]*what / how / who* nice!
SAM And [7]*she is / it is / this is* my wife, Jackie.
JAMES Your wife – wow! That's fantastic [8]*new / news / notices*! Nice to [9]*meet / meat / meeting* you, Jackie.
JACKIE Nice to meet you, [10]*two / too / to.*

b 01.03 Listen and check.

c Complete the sentences with the words in the box.

surprise	hello	meet	news	again
time	last	~~nice~~	must	up

1 Sea View Road? Oh, how *nice*!
2 Your husband – wow! That's fantastic ________!
3 We really ________ go. We're late.
4 What a lovely ________!
5 Say ________ to Roger for me.
6 Long ________ no see!
7 It was really nice to ________ you.
8 We must meet ________ soon.
9 It was great to see you ________.
10 When did we ________ see each other?

d 01.04 Listen and check.

2 PRONUNCIATION

Sentence stress

a 01.05 Listen to the sentences and underline the stressed words.

1 I'm pretty sure it was two months ago.
2 What a lovely surprise!
3 It was really nice to meet you.
4 I'm sorry, but I really must go.
5 Where are you living these days?
6 I'm late for a meeting.

1D SKILLS FOR WRITING
I'm sending you some photos

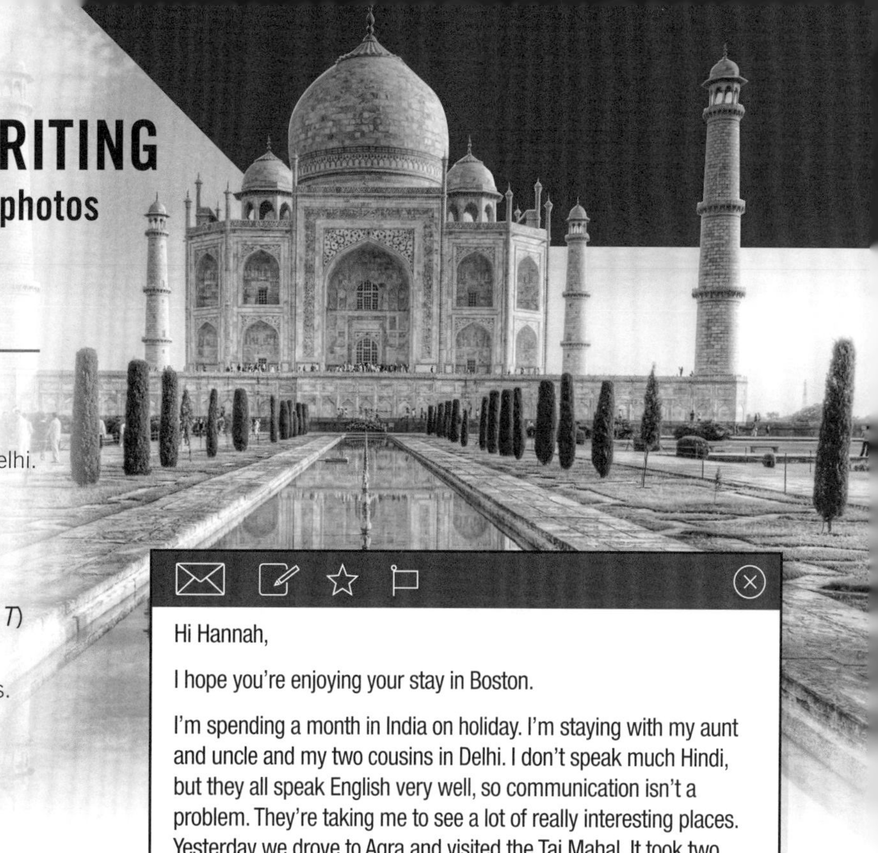

1 READING

a Read Nandeep's email to Hannah and tick (✓) the correct answer.

a ☐ Nandeep is staying at the Taj Mahal hotel in Delhi.
b ☐ Nandeep is visiting his cousins in Boston.
c ☐ Nandeep is on holiday at his aunt and uncle's house in Delhi.

b Read the email again. Are the sentences true (*T*) or false (*F*)?

1 ☐ Nandeep mainly speaks in Hindi to his cousins.
2 ☐ He's visiting a lot of places while he's in India.
3 ☐ The Taj Mahal is in Delhi.
4 ☐ Nandeep didn't enjoy visiting the Taj Mahal.
5 ☐ Nandeep often uses his aunt and uncle's pool.
6 ☐ Nandeep isn't enjoying his holiday.

Hi Hannah,

I hope you're enjoying your stay in Boston.

I'm spending a month in India on holiday. I'm staying with my aunt and uncle and my two cousins in Delhi. I don't speak much Hindi, but they all speak English very well, so communication isn't a problem. They're taking me to see a lot of really interesting places. Yesterday we drove to Agra and visited the Taj Mahal. It took two hours to get there. This is a photo I took – what an amazing building!

It's really hot here all the time, but my aunt and uncle have a swimming pool, so we spend a lot of our time in the water – it's so relaxing! In the evening, I usually go to cafés with my cousins and their friends.

I'm having a great time here in India!

See you soon.

Nandeep

2 WRITING SKILLS
Correcting mistakes

a Correct the sentences.

1 I'm having a lovely time here in france.
I'm having a lovely time here in France.
2 Yesterday we visitted the Palace of Versailles near Paris.
______
3 In the mornings, I usually going to the beach with my Portuguese friends.
______
4 I hope your having a great time in Canada with your family.
______
5 Their English are very good, but we always speak in German.
______

3 WRITING

a Read the email from Paul. Use the notes in brackets to write Maria's reply.

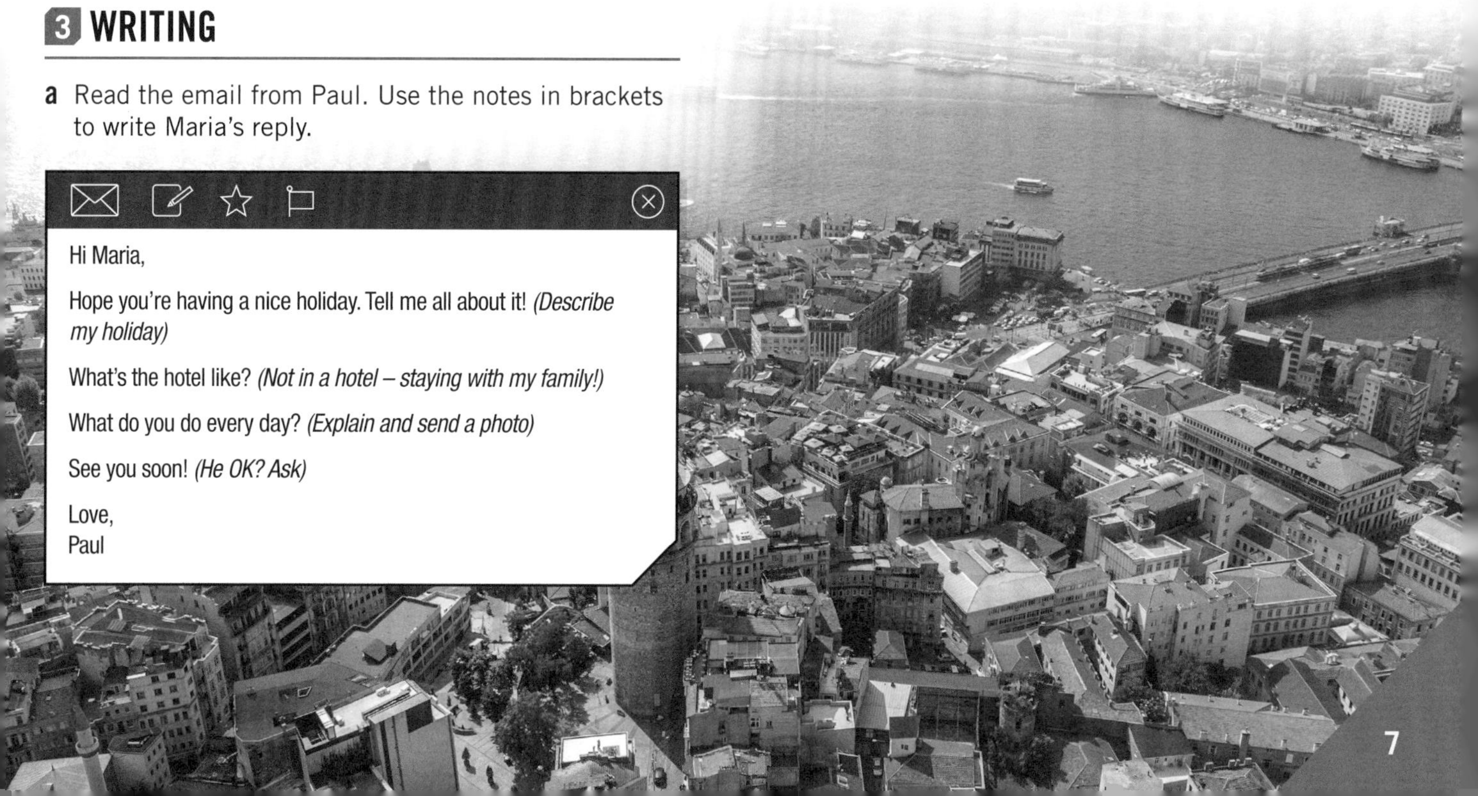

Hi Maria,

Hope you're having a nice holiday. Tell me all about it! *(Describe my holiday)*

What's the hotel like? *(Not in a hotel – staying with my family!)*

What do you do every day? *(Explain and send a photo)*

See you soon! *(He OK? Ask)*

Love,
Paul

UNIT 1
Reading and listening extension

1 READING

a Read the article. Match the statements 1–3 with the people a–c.

1 Living abroad is different from living in the UK — b
2 Not everyone would love working abroad.
3 It's important to see new places often.

a Vanessa
b Tony
c Emma

WORKING ABROAD: IS IT FOR YOU?

Are you looking for a new challenge at work? Do you want to meet new people and travel? Lots of people work abroad to experience a new culture. British people especially have a positive experience – 74% of Brits who live abroad say they feel at home in their new country! I talked to some young people from the UK about their experiences.

EMMA, 27, MEXICO CITY

I work as an English teacher in Mexico City. It's an amazing city! It's cheap to live here, so I'm saving quite a lot of money. Working abroad is not for everyone. I love Mexico, but I miss home too. My plan is to return home in three months. One year abroad is enough for me!

VANESSA, 25, BERLIN

I've been in Berlin for two years. I work in IT. My job is sometimes boring, but the city is exciting! I've also travelled to other parts of the country. It's easy to travel around Germany, so I try to see a new city or town once a month. I'd like to stay here for a long time and never stop seeing new places.

TONY, 24, PARIS

Living in Paris is very different from back home, but I love my life here. I'm studying basic French and working as an event planner for a British company. I travel all over Europe for work and have friends and colleagues in many countries – my life is very exciting!

You might face some problems living abroad, but a lot of people are doing it these days. It helps you grow professionally and personally. Why don't you see what opportunities are outside your country?

b Read the article again and tick (✓) the best endings for the sentences.

1 British people living abroad …
   a ☐ rarely feel comfortable in their new countries.
   b ☑ often have a positive experience.
   c ☐ always want to return home after a year.
2 Emma …
   a ☐ has been in Mexico for three months.
   b ☐ thinks Mexico City is wonderful.
   c ☐ wants to stay abroad more than a year.
3 Vanessa …
   a ☐ thinks that Berlin is a cheap city.
   b ☐ thinks her job is exciting.
   c ☐ often travels outside Berlin.
4 Tony …
   a ☐ doesn't speak a lot of French.
   b ☐ works with only British people.
   c ☐ travels outside Europe for work.
5 The writer of the article thinks that …
   a ☐ living abroad is easy.
   b ☐ living abroad can help you with future jobs.
   c ☐ there are many opportunities to work abroad.

c Write a paragraph about the advantages and disadvantages of living and working abroad. Think about:

- family and friends
- possible problems with the new language and culture
- the stories in the article
- your own experience.

2 LISTENING

a 01.06 Listen to the podcast. Match 1–3 with a–c to make true sentences.

1 Sophia — a goes to a club every week.
2 Ollie — b is friends with the people he lives with.
3 Ethan — c meets people in a café every week.

b 01.06 Listen to the podcast again and tick (✓) the best endings for the sentences.

1 The podcast is about …
- a [ ] starting university.
- b [ ] moving to a new city.
- c [✓] how people make friends.

2 Ollie doesn't …
- a [ ] usually go to bars.
- b [ ] like making friends with new people.
- c [ ] find it difficult to meet people at university.

3 Ollie likes …
- a [ ] going to parties with his friends.
- b [ ] people who like similar things to him.
- c [ ] the countryside near where he lives.

4 Sophia is interested in …
- a [ ] making friends with people studying drama.
- b [ ] joining a club.
- c [ ] meeting a lot of different people.

5 Ethan doesn't …
- a [ ] use the Internet to meet people.
- b [ ] like the people he lives with.
- c [ ] usually go out in the evening.

6 Which of the sentences is true about the students?
- a [ ] The university is helping all the students make friends.
- b [ ] The students are making friends in different ways.

c Write questions and answers about what you do in your free time and who you spend it with. Think about these questions:

- Where do you spend your free time?
- What do you do and how often?
- Who do you spend your free time with?

Review and extension

1 GRAMMAR

Correct the sentences.

1 Where you went on holiday last year?
Where did you go on holiday last year?
2 At the moment, she works in the café by the bus station.
3 Why you missed the bus?
4 I can't talk to you now because I do my homework.
5 What kind of music you usually listen to?
6 They waiting for the coach to London.

2 VOCABULARY

Correct the sentences.

1 The new Batman film is amaizing!
The new Batman film is amazing!
2 We very enjoyed the film last night.
3 We had a luvly time at the party last night.
4 I think our history lessons are so borring.
5 I think that man's a bit extrange. Look, he's talking to himself.
6 New York's allright, but I prefer living in London, actually.

3 WORDPOWER *like*

Match 1–8 with a–h to make sentences.

1 [e] We can go for a walk in the park
2 [ ] What was the party
3 [ ] What amazing weather! It looks
4 [ ] The boy in the white T-shirt looks
5 [ ] He loves films with superheroes, you know,
6 [ ] I absolutely love this singer. She sounds
7 [ ] I want to buy a computer
8 [ ] Thanks for your email. It sounds

a like a perfect day for the beach.
b like this one. How much is it?
c like Jacob. They've got the same smile.
d like you're having a great holiday.
e if you like.
f like Katy Perry.
g like Batman and Spider-Man.
h like last night?

REVIEW YOUR PROGRESS

Look again at Review Your Progress on p. 16 of the Student's Book. How well can you do these things now?
3 = very well 2 = well 1 = not so well

I CAN …	
ask and answer personal questions	[ ]
talk about how I communicate	[ ]
greet people and end conversations	[ ]
write a personal email.	[ ]

2A WE HAD AN ADVENTURE

1 GRAMMAR Past simple

a Tick (✓) the correct sentences. Correct the wrong sentences.

1 ☐ The train not arrived until 10:30 pm, so we got home around midnight.
The train didn't arrive until 10:30 pm, so we got home around midnight.

2 ☐ I slept very badly on the plane, so I feeled very tired the next day.
____

3 ☐ Did you took the train from New York to Washington?
____

4 ☐ We flew from London to Manchester because it was really cheap.
____

5 ☐ They spended two nights in a hotel and then they stayed at a friend's house for three days.
____

6 ☐ I didn't enjoyed my trip to Scotland because the weather wasn't very good.
____

7 ☐ When I got back to my hotel, I got a text from my sister.
____

8 ☐ We unpacked our suitcases and ate dinner in the hotel restaurant. It cost 100 euros!
____

b Complete the exchanges with the past simple form of the verbs in brackets. Use contractions where possible.

1 **A** How *was* (be) your flight?
B Fine, thanks, but I ________ (not sleep) because the seats ________ (not be) comfortable.

2 **A** What ________ (you, do) last summer?
B We ________ (not have) much money, so we ________ (decide) to stay in the UK.

3 **A** Where ________ (Ben, go) on holiday last year?
B He ________ (go) to Canada.

4 **A** ________ (you, bring) back any souvenirs from Jamaica?
B Yes, I ________. (do) I ________ (buy) some Blue Mountain coffee.

5 **A** ________ (you, see) your French friends when you were in Paris?
B Yes, we ________. (do) We ________ (meet) them for dinner one evening.

6 **A** ________ (you, visit) your cousins in Los Angeles?
B No, we ________ (not have) time.

2 VOCABULARY Tourism

a Match 1–8 with a–h to make sentences.

1 [d] We decided to go to China on holiday, so we had to get
2 ☐ I'm really bored. Why don't we do
3 ☐ James decided to go away
4 ☐ Going to the Olympics is great, but you need to book
5 ☐ It's a good idea to buy
6 ☐ Come on! Let's unpack
7 ☐ My daughter didn't have much money, so she stayed
8 ☐ On the day you leave, you need to check out of

a to Scotland for the weekend.
b our suitcases and go out for lunch.
c in hostels when she went travelling for a year.
d a visa from the embassy.
e some sightseeing this afternoon?
f your accommodation before you go.
g your hotel by 11 o'clock.
h souvenirs here – they're very expensive at the airport.

b Write the names of the holiday items under the pictures.

1 *suntan lotion*

2 ________

3 ________

4 ________

5 ________

6 ________

3 PRONUNCIATION *-ed* endings

a Tick (✓) the verbs that have an extra syllable when we add *-ed*.

Infinitive	+ *-ed*	Extra syllable?
depart	departed	✓
love	loved	
listen	listened	
hate	hated	
sound	sounded	
look	looked	
post	posted	
invite	invited	
enjoy	enjoyed	
like	liked	

b 02.01 Listen and check.

2B EVERYONE WAS WAITING FOR ME

1 VOCABULARY Travel collocations

a Complete the sentences with the correct forms of the verbs in the box.

miss take off get to change give
land leave for board ~~travel around~~

When I was a student, my best friend and I [1]travelled around Europe for a month. We rented a car and [2]__________ other travellers a lift using a ride-sharing app. It was a great way to save money and meet people!

She [3]__________ her holiday at six o'clock in the morning. However, she [4]__________ the 6:30 train because there was a traffic jam in the city centre.

Our plane [5]__________ from Beijing 45 minutes late but we [6]__________ in Sydney ten minutes early!

Our journey from London to Glasgow was terrible! We [7]__________ our train in London at two o'clock but then we [8]__________ trains in Birmingham and also in Manchester. In the end, we [9]__________ Glasgow just after midnight!

b Underline the correct words to complete the sentences.

1 **A** Why was there a big *strike* / *traffic jam* / *lift* on the motorway this morning?
  B Because there was a two-car *crash* / *strike* / *queue* at 7:30.
2 **A** Why did you *lose* / *miss* / *delay* your train?
  B Well, my friend was driving us to the station but her GPS device gave us the wrong directions, so we *left* / *broke down* / *got lost*. In the end, we asked someone for help!
3 **A** Why were there *traffic jams* / *long delays* / *crashes* for all the flights from Heathrow Airport today?
  B Because there was a pilots' *strike* / *turbulence* / *delay* yesterday, so a lot of planes are at the wrong airport today.
4 There was *turbulence* / *something wrong* / *a strike* with our bus, so we waited for two hours at the bus station.
5 It took me over an hour to get my ticket because there was a long *delay* / *queue* / *crash* at the ticket office. Then the train *got lost* / *took off* / *broke down* just outside Paris, so that's why I'm so late.
6 **A** It sounds like you had a bad flight between Washington and London.
  B Yes, there was a lot of *turbulence* / *queues* / *strikes* over the Atlantic because of the bad weather.

2 GRAMMAR Past continuous

a Complete the sentences with the past continuous forms of the verbs in brackets.

1 When we arrived at the station, my uncle was waiting for us in the car park. (wait)
2 It __________ hard when we got to our hotel. (snow)
3 __________ over the Alps when the turbulence started? (you, fly)
4 How fast __________ when the accident happened? (you, drive)
5 Where __________ when the thief stole your handbag? (you, stand)
6 Did you get lost because your GPS __________ ? (not work)

b Complete the text with the past simple or past continuous forms of the verbs in brackets.

My mother and I [1]had (have) a terrible journey from London to Edinburgh last weekend. First, when my brother [2]__________ (drive) us to the airport on Saturday evening, his car [3]__________ (break down) on the motorway. In the end, we [4]__________ (miss) our flight, so we [5]__________ (buy) some new tickets for the flight on Sunday morning instead. However, on Sunday morning we [6]__________ (wait) for our flight when it [7]__________ (start) snowing heavily, and they [8]__________ (decide) to close the airport. So we [9]__________ (take) a taxi to the station and [10]__________ (buy) tickets for the 2 pm train.

3 PRONUNCIATION Vowel sounds

a 02.02 Listen to the sentences. Do the letters in **bold** sound like /ə/ as in *computer*, /ɒ/ as in *dog* or /ɜː/ as in *her*? Tick (✓) the correct box for each sentence.

	Sound 1 /ə/ (e.g. *comput**er***)	Sound 2 /ɒ/ (e.g. *d**o**g*)	Sound 3 /ɜː/ (e.g. *h**er***)
a W**er**e you waiting for the bus?	✓		
b I w**a**sn't driving the car.			
c They w**er**e watching TV.			
d We w**er**en't having dinner.			
e She w**a**s talking on her phone.			
f W**a**s she listening?			
g He w**a**sn't smoking.			
h They w**er**en't playing chess.			

2C EVERYDAY ENGLISH

What time's the next train?

1 USEFUL LANGUAGE
Asking for information in a public place

a Put the words in the correct order to make questions.

1 anything else / help you / with / I / there / is / can ?
Is there anything else I can help you with?
2 is / tell / where / information desk / you / me / the / could ?
____
3 Edinburgh / to / much / is / a return ticket / how ?
____
4 for the airport / leave / do / often / buses / how / the ?
____
5 Barcelona / time / the next coach / what / to / is ?
____
6 my ticket / pay / euros / can / for / in / I ?
____
7 can / a sandwich / the journey / for / where / buy / I ?
____
8 a taxi / to the airport / much / it / does / cost / to get / how ?
____

b 02.03 Listen and check.

c Complete the conversation with the words in the box.

can near here have over there could you ~~excuse~~
anything else actually from what time

A [1] *Excuse* me.
B Yes, how [2]________ I help you?
A [3]________ tell me which platform the next train to London leaves [4]________?
B Certainly, madam. It leaves from platform 2.
A OK, thanks. And [5]________ does it leave?
B It leaves at 10:32, in 12 minutes.
A Brilliant. Thanks.
B Is there [6]________ I can help you with?
A [7]________, there is one more thing. Where can I buy a cup of coffee? Is there a café [8]________ ?
B Yes, there is. There's a café on the platform, [9]________.
A Brilliant. Thanks so much.
B No problem. [10]________ a good journey.

d 02.04 Listen and check.

e Match the traveller's sentences 1–8 with the ticket seller's responses a–h.

1 [c] Hello.
2 [ ] Could you tell me what time the next bus to Folkstone leaves, please?
3 [ ] Great, thanks! And where does it leave from?
4 [ ] I will be. Can I have a ticket, please?
5 [ ] Here you are. Also, is there somewhere I can buy a newspaper?
6 [ ] That's OK. I can run fast.
7 [ ] Yes, I think that's it. Thank you for your help!
8 [ ] Thanks! Bye!

a Goodbye!
b Yes, of course. It leaves in five minutes.
c Good afternoon. How can I help you?
d Certainly. That'll be £9.50.
e No problem, sir. Now hurry, or you'll miss your bus!
f From gate number 4, but you'll need to be quick!
g You'll need to! Is that all, sir?
h Yes, at the newsagent over there, but I'm not sure you'll have time.

2 PRONUNCIATION Connected speech

a 02.05 Listen to the questions. Tick (✓) the two words that are joined together.

1 When did you check into your hotel?
a [✓] che**ck in**to b [ ] you**r h**otel
2 How can I help you?
a [ ] ca**n I** b [ ] hel**p y**ou
3 Did you get a visa when you went to China?
a [ ] ge**t a** b [ ] whe**n y**ou
4 What time did you set off from home?
a [ ] di**d y**ou b [ ] se**t o**ff
5 What time is your plane?
a [ ] ti**me i**s b [ ] i**s y**our
6 How much is a return ticket to Bath?
a [ ] mu**ch i**s b [ ] t**o B**ath

2D SKILLS FOR WRITING
This city is different, but very friendly

1 READING

a Read Roberto's blog and tick (✓) the correct answers.

1 Roberto and Ana are staying in …
  a ☐ a hotel in the centre of London.
  b ☐ a hostel near Heathrow Airport.
  c ☐ a hotel in Earl's Court.
  d ☐ a hostel near the centre of London.

2 On Sunday, Roberto and Ana …
  a ☐ had fish and chips for lunch.
  b ☐ spent all day at the British Museum.
  c ☐ went to the British Museum and Covent Garden.
  d ☐ thought the British Museum was boring.

SATURDAY

Ana and I got to London at 11:30 this morning. It was a very long flight from São Paulo. When we got off the plane, the first thing we noticed was the cold – six degrees! I'm glad I brought a warm coat! In São Paulo, it was 35 degrees when we left. Everything they say about Londoners is true! The people at the airport weren't very friendly and they couldn't understand our English. And we couldn't understand what they were saying. In the end, we took the Underground from Heathrow Airport to our hostel in Earl's Court, near the centre of London. The hostel is full of young tourists from all over the world and everyone was very friendly and helpful. We were very tired, so we decided to sleep for a few hours. Ana's telling me to get ready to go and eat, so I have to finish now – more tomorrow.

SUNDAY

Ana and I had our first experience of British food last night. We went to a little café near the hostel. We decided to try fish and chips. It's a typical British dish and it was delicious with a hot cup of tea (with milk!). Today we visited the British Museum and Covent Garden. The British Museum is amazing – there are lots of interesting things to see. We spent two hours there and only saw a few of the rooms. We bought some sandwiches for lunch and then we went to Covent Garden market. There were lots of musicians and magicians in the street. We had a lovely afternoon and Ana took a lot of photos. You can see them on Facebook.

b Read the blog again. Are the sentences (*T*) true or false (*F*)?

1 ☐ On Saturday, it was warmer in London than in São Paulo.
2 ☐ It was difficult for Roberto and Ana to understand the people at the airport.
3 ☐ When they got to the hostel, they went to bed.
4 ☐ They didn't enjoy their fish and chips.
5 ☐ They didn't see all the rooms in the British Museum.
6 ☐ They had lunch in a restaurant in Covent Garden.

2 WRITING SKILLS Linking words

a Underline the correct words to complete the sentences.

1 There was a long queue for the museum, *and* / *so* / *but* we decided to go to the market instead.
2 We didn't visit the Tower of London *because* / *so* / *but* the tickets were very expensive.
3 The hotel looked really nice, *because* / *and* / *but* they didn't have any available rooms that night.
4 Yesterday I visited Ellis Island *so* / *and* / *because* the Statue of Liberty.
5 There weren't any flights today *but* / *so* / *because* there was a snowstorm.
6 *Because* / *When* / *So* we got to our hotel, I called my wife to wish her 'Happy Birthday'.
7 It started raining hard, *but* / *because* / *so* we didn't go to the mountains.
8 We wanted to go to the concert, *but* / *so* / *because* we couldn't get any tickets.

3 WRITING

a Read the notes. Write Maite's blog post about her holiday in New York.

Maite's blog: New York post (notes)

Monday, January 25
Madrid: left 12:20
New York: arrived 14:30
Very tired – (why?)
Weather: very cold – minus 6 degrees!
People = (?)
Hotel = (?)
Dinner = (?)

UNIT 2
Reading and listening extension

1 READING

a Read the article. How did the couples travel? Tick (✓) the correct ways. Sometimes there is more than one possible answer.

1 Carl and Sam
- a ☐ on foot
- b ☑ on two wheels
- c ☑ on four wheels
- d ☐ by boat

2 Ashish and Bryony
- a ☐ on foot
- b ☐ on two wheels
- c ☐ on four wheels
- d ☐ by boat

3 Yvette and Rob
- a ☐ on foot
- b ☐ on two wheels
- c ☐ on four wheels
- d ☐ by boat

b Read the article again and underline the correct names to complete the sentences.

1 *Carl and Sam / Ashish and Bryony / Yvette and Rob* stayed in Bristol for most of the week.
2 *Carl and Sam / Ashish and Bryony / Yvette and Rob* enjoyed the first day of the race.
3 *Carl and Sam / Ashish and Bryony / Yvette and Rob* stopped when they didn't know where they were.
4 *Carl and Sam / Ashish and Bryony / Yvette and Rob* finished their trip on foot when something happened to the vehicle they were in.
5 *Carl and Sam / Ashish and Bryony / Yvette and Rob* stopped after the first day.

c Complete the words to make sentences about the article. Write one word in each space.

1 During the race, the students couldn't ________ spend any money.
2 When they started the race, the weather was s________.
3 Carl and Sam got a l________ home with Carl's dad.
4 It c________ money for Ashish and Bryony to stay at a hotel.
5 Yvette and Rob got to Spain early in the m________.

d Write about a long journey you went on. Remember to include:

- where you went
- a description of how you travelled there
- what you thought of the place.

In July, a group of students from Bristol University, England, had a race. It started at the university at 9 am on 20th July. The winners were the pair who travelled the longest distance in seven days without spending any money.

CARL AND SAM

We decided to cycle. The sun was shining when we left and it was fun. But on the third day, it started raining and we got lost. It was awful. We slept under a tree in a field. The next morning Carl called his dad, and he came to get us and drove us home.

Distance travelled: 110 miles

ASHISH AND BRYONY

A friend gave us a lift on her way to her parents' house, but there were long delays and we didn't go far for hours. That evening as we were driving north, her car broke down and we had to get out. We didn't know what to do. We were tired and hungry, so we decided to walk to a village and stay in a hotel. But we had to pay. The next day, we went home.

Distance travelled: 130 miles

YVETTE AND ROB

We decided to walk to the port in Bristol and try to board a ship. We went to the office and asked if any ships would take us for free. For four days no one would. On the fifth day, we found a ship to take us to Spain. We boarded the ship and two days later we arrived in Bilbao as the sun was rising. It was amazing.

Distance travelled: 640 miles

2 LISTENING

a ▶ 02.06 Listen to the conversation. Match problems a–e with where they are happening 1–5.

1 M3 ————	a crash and delays
2 M4	b long delays
3 M1	c no delays
4 Trains	d problems this weekend
5 Gatwick	e traffic jam

b ▶ 02.06 Listen to the conversation again and tick (✓) the correct answers.

1 Why were there delays on the M3 this morning?
   a ☑ There was a crash.
   b ☐ The police closed the road.
   c ☐ It was raining.

2 What happened three hours ago near Swindon?
   a ☐ There was an accident.
   b ☐ There was a very long queue of cars.
   c ☐ A lorry stopped working.

3 Who should use the A429 this evening?
   a ☐ people who are going to Swindon
   b ☐ lorries
   c ☐ everyone on the M4

4 People going to the music festival in Leeds tomorrow
   a ☐ should expect delays on the M1.
   b ☐ should check the traffic tomorrow.
   c ☐ can use the M1 without delays.

5 What is unusual about the trains today?
   a ☐ There aren't any trains working.
   b ☐ The trains are mainly working well.
   c ☐ There are lots of delays.

6 Where did Jackie and Bob stay last night?
   a ☐ in a hotel at the airport
   b ☐ on the floor at the airport
   c ☐ in India

c Write about a long journey you took. Remember to include:

- how you travelled
- how long it took
- what problems you had.

Review and extension

1 GRAMMAR

Correct the sentences.

1 When I did some housework, I heard the news on the radio.
   When I was doing some housework, I heard the news on the radio.
2 When we were getting to the station, the train was just arriving.
3 My wife called me while I waited for my plane.
4 A man was taking my wallet while I was in the queue for my ticket.
5 Last year, we were going on holiday to Greece for two weeks.
6 I was driving to the airport when I was seeing the accident.

2 VOCABULARY

Correct the sentences.

1 They missed their flight because Rob's car broke on the way to the airport.
   They missed their flight because Rob's car broke down on the way to the airport.
2 My travel from Berlin to London took 15 hours.
3 Last week, I went to Rome on a business travel.
4 The trafic was terrible because it was rush hour.
5 By the time they checked away the hotel, it was 2 pm.
6 In the afternoon, they went sighseeing in the old town.

3 WORDPOWER *off*

Complete the sentences with the words in the box.

75% I'm cut ~~turned~~ drove took are fell

1 He was tired when he went to bed, so he *turned* off the light and went to sleep.
2 Paul ________ off a piece of bread for me so I could try it.
3 When I got to the hotel, I ________ off my shoes.
4 She ________ off her motorbike and broke her arm.
5 Those jeans are cheap! There's ________ off the original price.
6 He got in his car and ________ off without speaking.
7 Good night. ________ off now. I'm meeting a friend.
8 Ladies and gentlemen: the film is about to start, so please make sure your phones ________ off.

REVIEW YOUR PROGRESS

Look again at Review Your Progress on p. 26 of the Student's Book. How well can you do these things now?
3 = very well 2 = well 1 = not so well

I CAN ...	
talk about past holidays	☐
describe travel problems	☐
ask for information in a public place	☐
write a travel blog.	☐

3A I'VE NEVER SEEN CROWDS LIKE THIS

1 GRAMMAR
Present perfect or past simple

a Put the words in the correct order to make sentences.

1 has / that old lady's / done / shopping / James / a lot of times.
<u>James has done that old lady's shopping a lot of times.</u>
2 you / have / to / been / in / Rio de Janeiro / the carnival / ever ?
____
3 and smartphone / I / TV / a new / bought / last week .
____
4 have / you / from / borrowed / money / me / never .
____
5 they / volunteer work / ever / done / have / any ?
____
6 big / never / a / for a waiter / left / tip / has / she .
____
7 money / have / any / you / homeless person / to / given / ever / a ?
____
8 several / I / found / last month / good bargains .
____

b Complete the exchanges with the present perfect or past simple forms of the words in brackets.

1 **A** <u>Have you ever given</u> money to charity? (you, ever, give)
B Yes, I __________ £10 to a cancer charity last week. (give)
2 **A** __________ for a discount in a shop before? (she, ever, ask)
B Yes, she __________ for a discount on some shoes and they offered her 10% off! (ask)
3 **A** __________ someone who was hurt? (you, ever, help)
B Yes, I __________ a woman who fell off her bike last week. (help)
4 **A** I __________ tips in that restaurant lots of times. (leave)
B Really? How much __________ the last time you went? (you, leave)
5 **A** __________ something online? (he, ever, buy)
B Yes, he __________ a new jacket that was in the sales last month. (buy)

2 VOCABULARY
Money and shopping

a Match 1–8 with a–h to make sentences.

1 [f] I follow my favourite shops on Instagram
2 [ ] That holiday sounds fantastic, but
3 [ ] My brother lent me £50 yesterday
4 [ ] If you can't afford to buy a new car,
5 [ ] She's just spent £150
6 [ ] I only buy clothes from that shop
7 [ ] If you buy two jackets,
8 [ ] When I borrow money

a so I could buy some new jeans.
b from my parents, I always pay it back quickly.
c when they have special offers.
d we can offer you a 20% discount.
e on two pairs of shoes.
f so I know when they have a sale.
g it costs £5,000 for just a week!
h why don't you get a loan from the bank?

b Complete the text with the words in the box.

into	afford	lend	spend	bank account
~~up for~~	borrow	back	loan	

I'm saving 1 <u>up for</u> a car at the moment. I put £200 2__________ my 3__________ every month. I can't 4__________ to buy a new car, so it will have to be second-hand – probably three or four years old. My parents have offered to 5__________ me some money but I don't want to 6__________ any money from them. They've just bought a very old house in the country and they need to 7__________ a lot of money on repairs. So I'm going to ask the bank for a 8__________ of £5,000. I think I can pay it 9__________ in two years.

3B I'VE ALREADY GIVEN £25 TO CHARITY

1 VOCABULARY
make / do / give collocations

a Match 1–8 with a–h to make sentences.

1 [d] She was very confident, so she made
2 [ ] When she read the email from her nephew, it made
3 [ ] Are you doing anything
4 [ ] He's a really funny guy. He always makes
5 [ ] Your daughter's very clever. Is she doing
6 [ ] My grandfather always gives us
7 [ ] We gave the tourists
8 [ ] He didn't use his camera any more, so he gave it

a away to his grandson.
b silly jokes when he's with friends.
c a big hug when we go to see him.
d a lot of friends at her new school.
e nice for your birthday?
f directions to the station.
g well at school this year?
h her smile because it was so funny.

b Underline the correct words to complete the sentences.

1 I love those old black-and-white films. Charlie Chaplin always *does* / *makes* / *gives* me smile.
2 You're so mean. You never *do* / *make* / *give* the waiters a tip.
3 He *made* / *did* / *gave* volunteer work for a charity in Africa last year.
4 She was so happy to see him again that she *gave* / *made* / *did* him a big hug.
5 Do your parents usually *make* / *give* / *do* something nice for their wedding anniversary?
6 I'm having a great time in Paris. I've *made* / *done* / *given* some new friends in the hostel.
7 The doctors say that she's *making* / *giving* / *doing* well and that she can leave hospital tomorrow.
8 I've never *made* / *given* / *done* anyone directions in Spanish – all the tourists who come here speak English.

2 GRAMMAR
Present perfect with *already* and *yet*

a Underline the correct adverb in each sentence.

1 Has she helped her sister with her homework *yet* / *already*?
2 Have you *already* / *yet* visited your grandmother this week?
3 He's *already* / *yet* done a great job, and it's only his second week with the company!
4 We haven't given away our old clothes *already* / *yet*.
5 Thanks for the invitation, but we've *already* / *yet* eaten dinner.
6 I haven't given her any advice *yet* / *already*, but I will if she asks me.
7 We haven't done that task *yet* / *already*. We need more time.
8 She's *already* / *yet* made a list of the things she needs.

b Correct the sentences.

1 Mike hasn't gone yet shopping.
Mike hasn't gone shopping yet.
2 He's made already a payment of £2,000.
____
3 Have you yet paid Louise back?
____
4 Eva already has spent the money she borrowed from me.
____
5 I haven't made yet any new friends at school.
____
6 Has she saved yet enough money to buy a new phone?
____
7 I've bought already a present for my wife.
____
8 Already they've given £1,000 to charity.
____

3C EVERYDAY ENGLISH
Do you have anything cheaper?

1 USEFUL LANGUAGE Talking to people in shops

a Put the conversation in the correct order.

- [ ] **B** Yes, I suppose she might like them. On second thoughts, maybe I should get something else.
- [1] **A** Good morning. Can I help you?
- [ ] **B** Do you have anything cheaper?
- [ ] **A** OK. Er, let me see … what about this necklace?
- [ ] **B** Yes, it's lovely. OK, I'll take it.
- [ ] **A** Are you looking for anything in particular?
- [ ] **B** Er, yes. I'm looking for a present for my mother.
- [ ] **A** Really? How about these earrings? They're really beautiful. A perfect present …
- [ ] **B** Well, she loves earrings.
- [ ] **A** Well, these earrings here are cheaper. They're only £50 with the discount.

b 03.01 Listen and check.

c Underline the correct words to complete the sentences.

1 How would you like to *cost* / *pay* / *buy*?
2 We're looking *for* / *at* / *after* a present for my grandfather.
3 Did you want something *on* / *in* / *at* particular?
4 Who's *then* / *after* / *next*, please?
5 *In second thoughts* / *On second thoughts* / *My second thought*, I really think we should get her a book.
6 Can you *enter* / *write* / *touch* your PIN, please?
7 Do you have this in a different *size* / *till* / *receipt*? Thanks.
8 Could you show us *something more* / *something else* / *something other*?

d Put the words in the correct order to make sentences.

1 for / jacket / looking / a / I'm .
I'm looking for a jacket.
2 a / 14 / size / I'm / I / think .
____
3 same / in / have / one / blue / do / the / you ?
____
4 much / tell / can / it / how / is / you / me ?
____
5 a bit / too / that's / expensive .
____
6 one / you / cheaper / do / have / a ?
____

2 PRONUNCIATION Sentence stress

a 03.02 Listen to the sentences and underline the stressed syllables or words.

1 Can you show us something else?
2 Can you enter your PIN, please?
3 I'm looking for a present for my husband.
4 Do you have any black jeans?
5 Thanks. I'll take it.
6 Actually, I think we should buy her a book.

3D SKILLS FOR WRITING
We've successfully raised £500

1 READING

a Read David and Philip's email and tick (✓) the correct answer.

David and Philip are writing to …

a ☐ ask their colleagues for more money.
b ☐ invite their colleagues to a party.
c ☐ tell their colleagues about Cancer Research and how they have all helped.
d ☐ ask their colleagues to swim a kilometre.

b Read David and Philip's email again. Are the sentences true (*T*) or false (*F*)?

1 ☐ In the last year, they have given £2,500 to Cancer Research.
2 ☐ In April, 30 people swam a kilometre to raise money.
3 ☐ The party in June was very popular.
4 ☐ Four thousand people with cancer get money from Cancer Research.

Hello everyone,

We'd like to say a big 'Thank you!' to everyone who has helped us raise money for Cancer Research over the past six months. We've successfully raised £2,500!

We really hope you have enjoyed the different events that we have organised this year. First, we had a 'Swimathon' in April. Thirty of us swam a kilometre and raised over £1,000. Then 200 people came to our fantastic summer party in June. And don't forget to come to our special quiz night in September. There are some amazing prizes!

Cancer Research will use the money to do important research. This includes the work of over 4,000 scientists, doctors and nurses who are fighting cancer in this country. Cancer Research helps thousands of people with cancer every year.

Would you like to help us raise more money for Cancer Research? Please look out for the next event. Thanks again for all your help.

David and Philip

2 WRITING SKILLS Paragraphing

a Read the sentences. Put them in the correct order to make an email with four paragraphs. The paragraphs should be in the following order:

- Introduction
- How the team has raised / raises money
- Information about ActionAid
- Closing the email

☐ Thanks again for all your help. Please look out for our next event.
☐ ActionAid will use the money to help poor people around the world, to educate them and to protect them. In the past ten years, they have helped thousands of children start school.
☐ We have successfully raised £750.
☐ And, of course, next Friday there is the book and calendar sale at lunchtime.
1 We'd like to thank everyone for helping to raise money for ActionAid over the past year.
☐ Most of you came to the 1970s party in September. A lot of people also came to our karaoke night in November.
☐ So remember that a small amount of money can make a big difference. For example, only £4 per week gives a child in Africa clean water, education and medicine.

3 WRITING

a Read the notes and write Sam's email to his colleagues about the Save the Children charity.

<u>*Email to colleagues about Save the Children*</u>

Introduction:
Thank you – everyone who helped raise money – past 12 months. How much?

How the team has raised money and future events:
September: sports day
October: 1990s karaoke evening
Next week: quiz night + prizes!

Information about Save the Children:
Our money = save children's lives + better future
Last year STC helped 10m children around the world
Small amount of money = big difference, e.g. £3 saves lives of 8 children with a stomach virus

Closing the email
Help raise more money for STC?
Email me for info about future events
Thanks again

UNIT 3
Reading and listening extension

1 READING

a Read the magazine article. Complete the sentences with the numbers in the box.

100 12 million 13 million ~~87 million~~

1 A company bought the website for £ 87 million .
2 He started the website with £________.
3 The website has more than ________ regular users.
4 Charities got £________ from Martin after he sold the website.

MARTIN LEWIS: THE MONEY MAN

Martin Lewis is a journalist, TV host and writer. He knows a lot about money: how to spend it, where to use it and most of all, how to save it!

Martin was always interested in saving money and helping other people save money. He gave tips to friends about it, he talked about it on television and he wrote about it in a national newspaper. In 2003, he decided to start a website. He paid a man in Uzbekistan £100 to design his website and soon thousands of people were using it. The website gave lots of useful information. It told people which times of the day supermarkets had the best offers. It helped people get discounts on everything from clothes to holidays. It told people when shops had sales. The website helped people buy things that they couldn't afford to buy before. And if you needed to borrow money to buy a new car or a house, it told you which banks were the best to lend it to you. A lot of people started using the site and started telling their friends about it.

The website has been a huge success and Martin has done very well. Over 13 million people now use it every month, and in 2012, Martin Lewis sold it to another company for £87 million. But Martin hasn't stopped helping people. Since selling the website, he has given away over £12 million to charities that help people look after their money. He's certainly made a lot of people smile. And it all started with £100.

b Read the magazine article again. Are the sentences true (*T*) or false (*F*)?

1 ☐ Martin Lewis is an expert on how to spend less money.
2 ☐ It took a long time before anyone used the website.
3 ☐ People can save money by going to supermarkets at a particular time of the day.
4 ☐ Martin Lewis still owns the website.
5 ☐ Martin's website made him a very rich man.

c Complete the summary of the magazine article with the correct forms of the verbs in the box.

borrow buy cost get
save spend ~~work~~ write

Before 2003, Martin Lewis [1] worked as a journalist and [2]________ about how to save money. In 2003, it [3]________ him £100 to start his website. Soon it was very popular. It has a lot of information about how to [4]________ less money in shops, how to open a bank account, how to [5]________ a discount on products and where to [6]________ money. The website has helped millions of people [7]________ money or get a loan since 2003. A company [8]________ the website in 2012 for £87 million.

d Write about something that you have borrowed from or lent to someone. Include answers to these questions:

- What was it?
- Who did you lend it to or borrow it from?
- For how long?

2 LISTENING

a ▶ 03.03 Listen to the conversation. Underline the correct names to complete the sentences.

1 *Anita* / *Gary* / *Mike* gave a man something that he didn't have.
2 *Anita* / *Gary* / *Mike* is helping a friend who doesn't have much money.
3 *Anita* / *Gary* / *Mike* does something nice for other people every week.
4 *Anita* / *Gary* / *Mike* asked other people to lend her things.
5 *Anita* / *Gary* / *Mike* made friends with someone after helping them.

b 03.03 Listen to the conversation again and tick (✓) the correct answers.

1 Why is Anita's neighbour having a party?
   a ☑ It's her daughter's birthday.
   b ☐ It's her son's birthday.
   c ☐ It's her husband's birthday.
2 Where is the birthday party going to be?
   a ☐ at the local beach
   b ☐ in the back garden
   c ☐ at the local park
3 What did the Greek man do?
   a ☐ He borrowed an umbrella from Gary.
   b ☐ He lent an umbrella to Gary.
   c ☐ He borrowed Gary's coat.
4 What happened when Gary saw the man again?
   a ☐ They had lunch.
   b ☐ They had a cup of tea.
   c ☐ They went on holiday together.
5 What has Gary just booked?
   a ☐ a ticket to the theatre
   b ☐ a flight to Liverpool
   c ☐ a flight to Greece
6 How does Mike try to make people smile?
   a ☐ He gives them balloons.
   b ☐ He tells them jokes.
   c ☐ He makes friends with them.

c Write about the nicest thing that you've ever done. Remember to include:

- who you helped
- why you helped them
- what you did
- how they felt and how you felt afterwards.

Review and extension

1 GRAMMAR

Correct the sentences.

1 I never left a big tip in a restaurant.
   I've never left a big tip in a restaurant.
2 Did you ever give money to charity?
3 I've been to China on business last year.
4 She already sold her old car.
5 I haven't bought yet a birthday present for my brother.
6 I already spent £200 this weekend.

2 VOCABULARY

Correct the sentences.

1 I've already opened an account bank in the UK.
   I've already opened a bank account in the UK.
2 Can you borrow me 50 euros, please?
3 I don't have a card credit, so I always pay with cash.
4 James is saving on for a new computer.
5 Our taxi driver was very friendly, so we made him a big tip.
6 I bought a new laptop in the sells – it was only £250!
7 Have you ever made any volunteer work?
8 Tony owes to me £50, but he hasn't paid it back yet.

3 WORDPOWER *just*

Complete the sentences with the words in the box.

about spoken in time like ~~leaving~~ a beginner over under

1 I'm just *leaving*. I'll be there in ten minutes!
2 There was a lot of traffic but we got to the airport just ________ for our flight.
3 My watch cost just ________ £200. Not cheap at all!
4 You're just ________ your mother – you have the same blue eyes!
5 Dinner is just ________ ready. It'll be five minutes.
6 The film is 125 minutes long. It's just ________ two hours.
7 I've just ________ to him. He'll meet us at 9:00.
8 No, she can't give a presentation in English yet. She's just ________.

REVIEW YOUR PROGRESS

Look again at Review Your Progress on p. 36 of the Student's Book. How well can you do these things now?
3 = very well 2 = well 1 = not so well

I CAN ...	
talk about money and shopping experiences	☐
talk about living with less	☐
talk to people in shops	☐
write an update email.	☐

4A I'M GOING TO THE HAIRDRESSER'S TOMORROW

1 VOCABULARY
Clothes and appearance

a Match the pictures with the words in the box.

underwear tights top tie high heels tracksuit ~~gloves~~ sandals earrings jumper flat shoes bracelet

1 _gloves_

2 ______

3 ______

4 ______

5 ______

6 ______

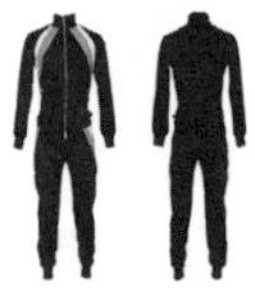

7 ______

8 ______

9 ______

10 ______

11 ______

12 ______

2 GRAMMAR
Present continuous and *be going to*

a Put the words in the correct order to make sentences.

1 buy / going / a new dress / I'm / the party / for / to .
I'm going to buy a new dress for the party.
2 going / your wedding / you / are / invite / your / to / cousin / to ?
______
3 aren't / going / they / get married / to / this / year .
______
4 going / are / do / after university / you / what / to ?
______
5 visit / Spain next year / going / we're / in / my relatives / to .
______
6 to / you / are / wear / to / the party / what / going ?
______

b Complete the conversation with the present continuous forms of the verbs in the box. Use contractions where possible.

stay come bring not fly ~~arrive~~ take meet (x2)

A So what have you arranged for this evening?
B Well, my parents [1] _are arriving_ at the station on the 6:30 train from Paris.
A So, [2] ______ you [3] ______ them at the station?
B Yes, we are. We [4] ______ a taxi from our house at 6:00. I booked it this morning.
A Good. So where [5] ______ they [6] ______?
B At the Hilton Hotel. They've got a double room with a balcony.
A Great. And what about the restaurant?
B I've reserved a table for eight at eight o'clock. Everyone [7] ______ to the restaurant at 7:45 so we can all be there when they arrive.
A Brilliant. Have you told the restaurant that it's your father's birthday?
B Yes, they've made him a special cake with HAPPY 60TH on it. They [8] ______ it to our table at ten o'clock, together with the coffee.
A And what about tomorrow?
B They [9] ______ to Scotland until the afternoon, so there's plenty of time. Their flight's at 3:30.
A Great, so it's all arranged. I have to go now because I [10] ______ Sally for a coffee in ten minutes. See you later!

c 04.01 Listen and check.

3 PRONUNCIATION
Sound and spelling: *going to*

a 04.02 Listen to *going to* in the sentences. Do you hear /ˈɡəʊɪŋ tə/ (*going to*) or /ɡənə/ (*gonna*)? Tick (✓) the correct box for each sentence.

	going to	*gonna*
1 Are you going to go out tonight?	☐	✓
2 What are you going to do for your birthday?	☐	☐
3 He isn't going to have a holiday this year.	☐	☐
4 We're going to try to find a taxi.	☐	☐
5 I'm going to have a shower after breakfast.	☐	☐
6 They aren't going to do their homework.	☐	☐
7 She's going to phone her brother.	☐	☐
8 I'm not going to go to Ibiza this year.	☐	☐

4B SHALL WE GO TO THE MARKET?

1 GRAMMAR
will / won't / shall

a Match 1–8 with a–h to make sentences.

1 [c] Let's go on holiday to Greece next summer.
2 [ ] You know I don't really like spicy food.
3 [ ] Which film shall we see with the kids?
4 [ ] Let's invite your parents for lunch next Sunday.
5 [ ] Hi. I'm at the supermarket, but I can't carry all the shopping on the bus.
6 [ ] Oh, no! We've just missed the last bus.
7 [ ] Hi, Dad. I'm afraid I've lost my mobile.
8 [ ] Oh, no. I haven't got enough money to buy this phone today.

a OK, shall I call a taxi?
b Good idea. I'll call them later to see if they're free.
c Good idea. I'll check flights and hotel prices tomorrow.
d Don't worry. I'll buy you a new one for your birthday.
e Oh, that's a pity. Shall I lend you some money?
f Don't worry. I'll bring the car and meet you there in ten minutes.
g Shall we go and see the new Disney film?
h OK, we won't go to an Indian restaurant.

b Underline the correct words to complete the sentences.

1 **A** *Will / Shall / Won't* we go to the cinema tonight?
B Yes, OK. I *'ll / won't / shall* check which films are on and call you back.
2 **A** Hi, Dad. I missed the last bus home!
B Don't worry. I *should / won't / 'll* bring the car and meet you at the cinema.
3 What *will / shall / won't* we do this weekend?
4 Don't worry. The station's very close to here, so you *'ll / shall / won't* miss your bus.
5 **A** *Shall / Will / Won't* we try to get tickets for the Imagine Dragons concert?
B Good idea. I *won't / shall / 'll* check prices online.
6 I know you're a vegetarian, so I'll / *won't / shall* cook steak for dinner.
7 *Will / Won't / Shall* you help me do the washing up?
8 **A** Let's take Monica and Sara to that new Chinese restaurant for dinner.
B Yes, that's a great idea. *Will / Won't / Shall* you call them and reserve a table for 7:30?

2 VOCABULARY Adjectives: places

a Complete the crossword puzzle.

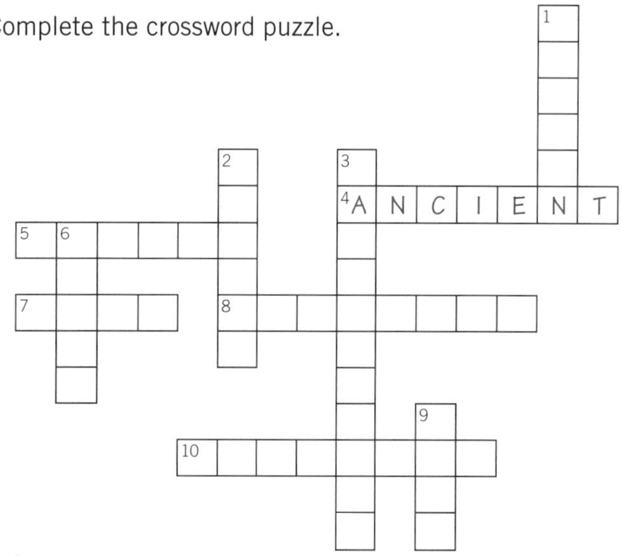

→ Across
4 Stonehenge is an *ancient* monument in Wiltshire in England. It's about 5,000 years old.
5 When the weather is really bad, we play on the i________ tennis court at my local gym.
7 There are a lot of h________ mountains in Switzerland. For example, the Matterhorn is about 4,500 metres above sea level.
8 I live in a very o________ town. Nothing interesting happens here!
10 We live in a p________ village. There's no traffic at all!

↓ Down
1 My school's in a really m________ building. It's only five years old.
2 This road is very n________. It isn't wide enough for a bus.
3 The view from the top of the Empire State Building is m________.
6 It's very n________ in this café, isn't it? It's difficult to hear you.
9 The British Museum is h________. There are almost 600 rooms!

b Choose the opposites of the adjectives in **bold**. Use the words in the box.

modern	high	pretty	outdoor	quiet	~~wide~~

1 The streets in the old part of town are very **narrow**. *wide*
2 I think the new houses they've built are really **ugly**. ________
3 There is a big **indoor** swimming pool in my town. ________
4 That restaurant's always very **noisy**. ________
5 This is one of the most **ancient** cities in Greece. ________
6 The hills in the South of England are quite **low**. ________

3 PRONUNCIATION
Sound and spelling: *want* and *won't*

a 04.03 Listen and underline the correct words to complete the sentences.

1 We *won't / want to* go swimming today.
2 They *want to / won't* take you to the old castle.
3 I *won't / want to* go to that restaurant again.
4 You *want to / won't* wait for the next train.
5 I *won't / want to* study English again next year.
6 Tom and I *want to / won't* invite him to our party.

4C EVERYDAY ENGLISH
Are you doing anything on Wednesday?

1 USEFUL LANGUAGE
Making arrangements

a Put the conversation in the correct order.

- [ ] **A** Oh, OK never mind. How about Friday? Is that OK for you?
- [ ] **B** Brilliant! 11 o'clock. See you then.
- [ ] **A** OK, so you can't do this week. What are you doing next Monday?
- [ ] **B** Oh, that sounds nice. I'll just check. No, sorry, I can't do Wednesday. I'm going shopping with my mother.
- [1] **A** Are you doing anything on Wednesday? Would you like to go for a coffee?
- [ ] **B** Next Monday? Just a moment, I'll just check. Nothing! I can do next Monday. Perfect!
- [ ] **A** Great! So we can meet for a coffee on Monday?
- [ ] **B** Friday … hang on a minute … no, sorry. I'm going to London for the day. This week's really busy for me.
- [ ] **A** Shall we meet at *The Coffee Place* at 11:00?
- [ ] **B** Yes, Monday's fine. Where shall we go?

b 04.04 Listen and check.

c Put the words in the correct order to make sentences.

1 like / would / bring / me / anything / you / to ?
Would you like me to bring anything?

2 anything / doing / you / Saturday / this / are ?
____

3 busy / us / week's / really / this / for .
____

4 come / we / what / round / shall / time ?
____

5 you / on / doing / next week / Tuesday / are / what ?
____

6 round / you / come / would / for / to / lunch / like ?
____

7 can't / Thursday / I / this week / do .
____

8 for / Sunday / is / OK / you / this ?
____

d 04.05 Listen and check.

Ana's calendar

Sunday	am	☆ day trip to Blackpool ☆
	lunch	
	pm	
Monday	am	9–11 meeting at work
	lunch	1–2 lunch with Mum
	pm	
Tuesday	am	7–9 aerobics class
	lunch	
	pm	6–8 cinema with Kemal
Wednesday	am	8–9 yoga
	lunch	
	pm	6:30 doctor's appointment
Thursday	am	
	lunch	12–1 shopping with Karen
	pm	7–8:30 dance class
Friday	am	all day – work conference
	lunch	
	pm	
Saturday	am	day off!
	lunch	
	pm	

e Read Ana's calendar and underline the correct words to complete the telephone conversation.

SANDRA Hi, Ana! Are you free to meet on Monday morning?
ANA Let me check my calendar. I'm sorry, I have [1] *an aerobics class / a meeting / a doctor's appointment* then.
SANDRA Oh, that's a pity. How about Monday for lunch?
ANA No, I'm having lunch with [2] *Kemal / my mum / Karen* then.
SANDRA Oh, well … are you doing anything on Tuesday evening?
ANA I'm afraid I'm going [3] *shopping / to the cinema / to a dance class*.
SANDRA That sounds like fun! Let's see. I'm busy on Wednesday and Thursday. Could we meet on Friday?
ANA Unfortunately, I'm busy all day on Friday. I have a [4] *doctor's appointment / dance class / work conference*.
SANDRA OK. What are you doing on Sunday?
ANA Oh dear. On Sunday I'm [5] *at a work conference / in Blackpool / in a meeting* all day.
SANDRA So you don't have any free time this week?
ANA Yes, I do! I have the whole day off on [6] *Wednesday / Thursday / Saturday*!

2 PRONUNCIATION Sentence stress

a 04.06 Listen to the sentences and underline the stressed words or syllables.

1 I can't meet you tomorrow.
2 He can meet us at the station.
3 I didn't understand him.
4 She hasn't seen that film.
5 I must start cooking dinner.
6 They don't like basketball.

4D SKILLS FOR WRITING
Are you free on Saturday?

1 READING

a Read Abby's email to Tony and his reply and tick (✓) the correct answer.

a ☐ Abby invites Tony and Laura to come to a birthday party at her house.
b ☐ Abby and Mike would like to go to a Chinese restaurant with Tony and Laura.
c ☐ Abby wants to see Tony and Laura's new house.
d ☐ Abby invites Tony and Laura to celebrate Mike's birthday at a Chinese restaurant.

Hi Tony,

How are things? We haven't seen you for ages. I hope you and Laura are well and enjoying your new house.

Are you doing anything on Friday, 21st June? It's Mike's 40th birthday and we're going to our favourite Chinese restaurant, *Xian*, with some friends. We're going to book a table for eight o'clock. Can you come? It would be lovely to see you both and have a chance to talk.

Everyone's bringing an old photo of Mike. Could you bring your favourite photo of Mike from when he was at school?

Love,

Abby

Hi Abby,

Great to hear from you. Yes, we're well and we love our new house. We've just finished painting our bedroom and we're going to start on the kitchen next weekend.

Thanks for inviting us to Mike's birthday party. We're free on the 21st and we'd love to come. I'll bring some really funny photos of Mike when he was at school! We're looking forward to seeing you and Mike.

All the best,

Tony

b Read the emails again. Are the sentences true (*T*) or false (*F*)?

1 ☐ Abby and Mike have seen Tony and Laura recently.
2 ☐ Tony and Laura have recently moved to a new house.
3 ☐ Abby wants Mike's friends to take photos of him at the restaurant.
4 ☐ Tony and Laura are making changes to their new house.
5 ☐ Tony doesn't have any old photos of Mike.

2 WRITING SKILLS Inviting and replying

a Correct the sentences. Use contractions where possible.

1 Hope your well and enjoying your new job.
Hope you're well and enjoying your new job.
2 Thanks for invite me to your party.
____
3 It would be great to seeing you.
____
4 We're free on Saturday and we love to come.
____
5 We having a party on Saturday.
____
6 We didn't see you for ages!
____

3 WRITING

a Read Sam's email to Olivia inviting her to his birthday party and the notes below. Decide whether Olivia can or can't go to the party and write her reply.

Hi Olivia,

How are you? I haven't seen you for over six months. I hope you are well and enjoying your new job.

Are you doing anything next Saturday? I'm having a birthday party at my house and I'm inviting a few friends. People are arriving at 7:30. Everyone is bringing some food for the party. Could you bring a salad?

It would be great to see you and catch up.

Love,

Sam

Notes for reply:
She CAN go to the party

1 Me? Fine. *Give information about new job*
2 Thanks for invitation
3 Free next Sat, love to come
4 Bring a huge salad!
5 Looking forward

Notes for reply:
She CAN'T go to the party

1 Me? Fine. *Give information about new job*
2 Thanks for invitation
3 Party = fun! Can't come
4 Visit cousin in Barcelona next weekend
5 Enjoy the party!

UNIT 4
Reading and listening extension

1 READING

a Read the magazine article. Put the events in the order that Julia does them.

- [ ] Arriving at the cinema
- [ ] Getting a new outfit
- [ ] Going to the hairdresser's
- [ ] Having lunch
- [ ] Meeting my friend
- [1] Running on Venice Beach

b Read the magazine article again. Are the sentences true (*T*) or false (*F*)?

1 [ ] There are a lot of people on Venice Beach in the morning.
2 [ ] Julia thinks she will spend all day shopping.
3 [ ] There are a lot of people at the shopping mall.
4 [ ] Julia doesn't want to have lunch until she's bought a new dress.
5 [ ] Julia is looking forward to the evening because she has never been to a premiere before.

c Complete the sentences with the correct forms of the verbs in brackets.

1 Julia _is meeting_ her friend at the shopping mall today. (meet)
2 At 1:15 Julia is ________ lunch. She ________ anything yet. (have, buy)
3 At 4:22 Julia ________ the hairdresser's in a taxi. (go)
4 At 6:35 Julia ________ to go out. (get ready)
5 At 7:15 she ________ at the cinema. (arrive)

d Write an email to a friend about your plans for the weekend. Remember to include:

- where you are going
- what you are going to do
- who you are going with
- what you think will happen.

12 HOURS IN LOS ANGELES
with film director Julia Fitzgerald

7:15 am The sun is shining and I'm going to put my tracksuit on and go for a run. I love this time of the day because it's so peaceful and quiet down on Venice Beach.

10:00 am I'm going to a film premiere tonight so I have to look my best. I've planned to meet my friend at an indoor shopping mall in Santa Monica, but she's not here yet. It's a modern place with a lot of great shops and some pretty little cafés. I'd like to buy a new dress. It's crowded today, so I'm sure we'll be here all day!

1:15 pm We've stopped for lunch at an ordinary LA restaurant. I haven't bought anything yet, but all this walking around is making me hungry. I'm going to get a burger and chips.

2:20 pm My friend's taking me to a huge new department store that sells everything. She thinks we'll find something there.

3:05 pm Success! I've found a gorgeous red dress and matching high heels. We've decided to celebrate with coffee and cake at my favourite outdoor café near the beach.

4:22 pm I'm in a taxi now. I have an appointment at the hairdresser's at 4:30 pm. I hope I'm not late, but I think I might be!

6:35 pm I'm nearly ready. Shall I wear the gold bracelet and necklace or the black one? I can't decide. The car is coming at 7:00 pm, so I have a bit of time.

7:15 pm We're driving up to the cinema for the premiere. It's crowded and noisy because everyone is hoping to see all the stars. It's my first time at a premiere so I'm really excited. It's going to be a wonderful night!

2 LISTENING

a 04.07 Listen to the conversation. Complete the sentences with the names in the box.

Alex Giles's mum Gavino ~~Giles~~ Isaac

1 *Giles* is going to finish university this summer.
2 ____________ is marrying an Italian woman.
3 ____________ is teaching Giles Italian next week.
4 ____________ wants to go sightseeing in Rome.
5 ____________ is going on a date tonight.

b 04.07 Listen to the conversation again and tick (✓) the correct answers.

1 Why is Giles going to Italy this summer?
   a ☑ He is going to a wedding.
   b ☐ His girlfriend is Italian.
   c ☐ He wants to visit Rome.
2 Who is Laura?
   a ☐ Giles's girlfriend
   b ☐ Alex's fiancée
   c ☐ a student in their class
3 What is Giles's dad going to do if Giles passes his exams?
   a ☐ He's going to pay for Italian lessons.
   b ☐ He's going to buy him a new suit.
   c ☐ He's going to take him to Rome.
4 What does Isaac like about Rome?
   a ☐ the new buildings
   b ☐ the history
   c ☐ the mix of old and new architecture
5 Where is Isaac going now?
   a ☐ He is going to work.
   b ☐ He is going to get a haircut.
   c ☐ He is going home.

c Write about what you're going to do when you finish your English course. Include answers to these questions:

- Where are you going to go?
- What would you like to do?

Review and extension

1 GRAMMAR

Correct the sentences.

1 I going to look for a job in a hotel this summer.
   I'm going to look for a job in a hotel this summer.
2 Don't worry. I pay the money back tomorrow.
3 He'll go to buy a new car next month.
4 Will I come to your house in half an hour?
5 Will we go to that café for a coffee?
6 Are you going to doing your homework this evening?

2 VOCABULARY

Correct the sentences.

1 There is a fantastic outside swimming pool in my town.
   There is a fantastic outdoor swimming pool in my town.
2 Are you going to buy a new suit case in the sales?
3 I love it here in the country. It's so peacefull!
4 He always uses a tie when he goes for a job interview.
5 I love coming to this park because you can't hear the traffic. It's so quite here.
6 That restaurant's so noise. It's really hard to talk there.

3 WORDPOWER *look*

Complete the sentences with the words in the box.

well forward up around ~~at~~ for

1 He looked *at* the timetable to see when the next train left for London.
2 Excuse me. I'm looking ____________ a bank. Is there one near here?
3 We're really looking ____________ to seeing our friends from Ecuador tomorrow.
4 Are you OK? You don't look ____________.
5 I'm tired! Do you really want to look ____________ the museum again?
6 If you aren't sure what it means, look ____________ the word in your dictionary.

REVIEW YOUR PROGRESS

Look again at Review Your Progress on p. 46 of the Student's Book. How well can you do these things now?
3 = very well 2 = well 1 = not so well

I CAN ...	
talk about plans for celebrations	☐
plan a day out in a city	☐
make social arrangements	☐
write and reply to an invitation.	☐

5A I HAVE TO WORK LONG HOURS

1 VOCABULARY Work

a Complete the sentences.

1 This person takes care of the plants and cuts the grass. gardener
2 When your hair gets too long, you make an appointment with this person. h__________
3 If you have a problem with your kitchen sink, you need to call this person. p__________
4 This person works in a laboratory and might have a university degree in chemistry or biology. s__________
5 Somebody whose job is to look after people's money. b__________
6 If you have a problem with the lights in your house, you call this person. e__________
7 If the police arrest you, this person can help you. l__________
8 This person can help you manage your money. a__________
9 This person cooks food in a restaurant. c__________
10 When you are in hospital, this person takes care of you. n__________

b Complete the sentences with the words in the box.

team people environment self-employed skills salary university degree qualifications training ~~long hours~~

1 He's usually in his office from 8 am until 8 pm, but he doesn't mind working long hours.
2 My sister works for a large bank in London. She has a very good __________ and drives a company car.
3 You need to have several years of __________ after you study to become a doctor.
4 They have a really nice working __________ – their offices are modern with air conditioning and plenty of light.
5 I really enjoy working on big projects with a lot of other people. It's good to work in a __________.
6 You need to have a __________ to become a lawyer.
7 Receptionists have to deal with __________, so they need to be friendly and polite.
8 Some people prefer to be __________ and work for a lot of different companies.
9 Secretaries need to have a lot of __________ – they need to be organised and good with computers.
10 You need to have good __________ if you want to get a job at this university.

2 GRAMMAR *must / have to / can*

a Complete the sentences about the signs with *have to* or *can't*.

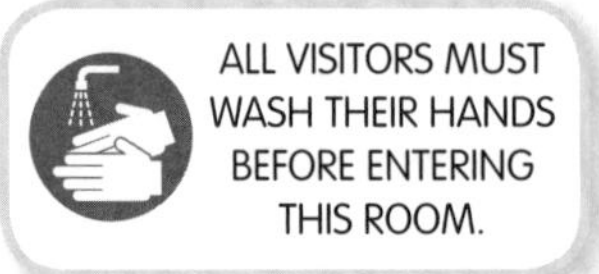

1 You have to wash your hands before you go into this room.

2 Excuse me, madam. You __________ stand up until the plane has stopped.

3 I'm sorry, sir. You __________ take photos in here with a flash.

4 Excuse me. I'm afraid you __________ wear your seat belt all the time.

5 Visitors __________ wear hard hats when they come to this building site.

6 I'm sorry. You __________ smoke in the toilet.

b Underline the correct words to complete the text.

I work as a receptionist in a big hotel, so I [1]*must / mustn't / can* always be polite to the guests. During the week, I [2]*don't have to / can't / must* go to bed late because I have to start work early. Fortunately, I [3]*don't have to / mustn't / can't* wear a uniform, but I [4]*can / mustn't / have to* dress smartly.

My sister's a student, so she [5]*mustn't / doesn't have to / can't* get up early most days. However, she [6]*doesn't have to / mustn't / has to* study very hard at the moment because she's got important exams next month.

My dad's a taxi driver, so he often [7]*has to / mustn't / can't* work in the evenings and at weekends. He [8]*doesn't have to / mustn't / must* drive fast because there are speed cameras everywhere in this city.

My mum's a nurse, so she [9]*has to / mustn't / can't* wear a uniform when she's at work. Sometimes she starts work very early, but my dad usually takes her to work in his taxi, so she [10]*must / doesn't have to / mustn't* take the bus.

5B I MIGHT GET A JOB TODAY!

1 GRAMMAR
will and *might* for predictions

a Match 1–8 with a–h to make sentences.

1 [c] She might
2 [ ] I think I'll
3 [ ] Spain might not
4 [ ] I don't think she'll
5 [ ] I'm sure he'll
6 [ ] France won't
7 [ ] He might not
8 [ ] I might not

a win the match on Saturday. The Brazilian team are just as good as them.
b pass his exams. He's very clever and he's worked really hard all year.
c feel better tomorrow. She says she's taken some medicine.
d get to school on time. I've only just woken up!
e pass his exams. He hasn't worked very hard this year.
f win the match on Saturday. They haven't got any good players in their team and Brazil are a fantastic team.
g come this evening. She's not feeling well.
h see them tonight. We all usually go to the gym on Thursdays.

b Complete the sentences with *will* (or *'ll*), *won't*, *might* or *might not*.

1 I'm sure you __will__ pass your exams. You've worked very hard this year.
2 Don't go on holiday next week. They ______ ask you back for a second interview.
3 I know they ______ offer me a good salary. A friend of mine works there and he doesn't earn a lot of money.
4 You ______ get a job immediately when you finish university – 50% of graduates don't have a job three years after finishing their studies.
5 She doesn't think she ______ go travelling after university. She wants to find a job as soon as possible.
6 **A** Do you think he ______ pass all his exams?
B Yes, I'm sure he ______. Don't worry.
7 Who knows? You ______ make some useful contacts at the conference.
8 I'm sure he ______ get the job. He doesn't have any experience.

2 VOCABULARY Jobs

a Write the names of the jobs under the pictures.

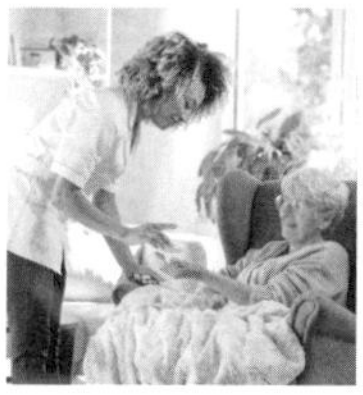
1 __carer__

2 ______

3 ______

4 ______

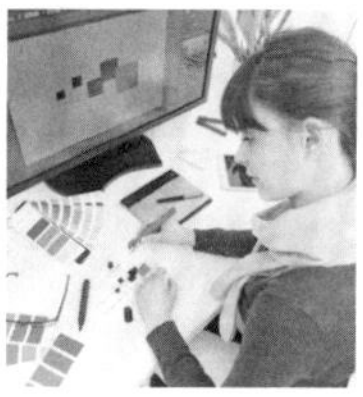
5 ______

6 ______

7 ______

8 ______

9 ______

10 ______

11 ______

12 ______

b Complete the sentences with the correct jobs.

1 When I was little, I wanted to be a v__et__ because I loved looking after animals.
2 I'm looking for a good b______ to fix the roof on my house.
3 Nick is a fantastic m______. He can play the piano, the guitar, the cello and the saxophone.
4 Christopher Wren was the a______ who designed St. Paul's Cathedral in London.
5 Michelle works in a department store as a s______ a______.
6 Chris Evans is an American a______, famous for his role as Captain America in the Marvel Comics films.
7 Adrian works as a c______, looking after old people in their homes.
8 Sarah works in our IT Department as a c______ p______.
9 James was a well-known j______ who worked for *The New York Times*.
10 Yves St. Laurent was a famous French fashion d______.
11 The t______ d______ works all over the city from 8 pm to 5 am.
12 I hope that the p______s in the UN can solve the world's problems one day.

5C EVERYDAY ENGLISH
I'll finish things here, if you want

1 USEFUL LANGUAGE
Offers and suggestions

a Put the words in the correct order to make sentences.

1 money / I / you / some / lend / the bus / for / shall ?
Shall I lend you some money for the bus?

2 off / maybe you / ask / manager / for / your / should / the day .

____

3 look up / the / I'll / train times / online .

____

4 do / a taxi / guest / you / our / me / to / want / for / call ?

____

5 drive / airport / don't / the / why / I / to / you ?

____

6 arranging / about / a / in / meeting / Mexico City / how ?

____

7 money / don't / why / borrow / from / some / you / your dad ?

____

8 Rome / could / direct flight / you / a / to / catch .

____

b 05.01 Listen and check.

c Complete the sentences with the words in the box.

fine about could mind ~~shall~~ sorry matter don't maybe would idea worry

1 **A** *Shall* I book a room for your meeting?
B Yes, good ______.
2 **A** ______ you like me to drive you to the station?
B No, I'll be ______. Don't ______ about it. I can walk.
3 **A** But you won't be able to have any lunch.
B Oh, never ______. I'm not really hungry.
4 **A** I'm really ______. I can't go to the cinema tonight.
B Oh, it doesn't ______. We can go another time.
5 How ______ asking your boss if you can have more time for the report?
6 Why ______ I book the train tickets online?
7 ______ you should invite your boss to the meeting, too.
8 You ______ send her some flowers for her birthday.

d 05.02 Listen and check.

2 PRONUNCIATION
Stressed/unstressed modals: vowel sounds

a 05.03 Listen to the sentences. Tick (✓) which vowel sounds you hear for the modal verbs in **bold**.

	Strong vowel /ʊ/	Weak vowel /ə/
1 **Would** you like a coffee?		✓
2 Yes, I **would**. Thanks.		
3 **Could** you help me with my report?		
4 Yes, of course I **could**.		
5 You **should** get a taxi.		
6 Yes, you're right. I **should**.		
	/æ/	/ə/
7 **Shall** I book a meeting room?		
8 Well, what do you think? **Shall** I?		

5D SKILLS FOR WRITING
I am writing to apply for a job

1 READING

a Read the job advert and Martin's job application, and tick (✓) the correct answer.

a ☐ The job is for 12 months.
b ☐ The job is in a hotel in Madrid.
c ☐ The hotel needs a receptionist.
d ☐ The hotel needs a waiter.

b Read the job advert and job application again. Are the sentences true (*T*) or false (*F*)?

1 ☐ The hotel will give the receptionist a bedroom and food.
2 ☐ People who apply for this job don't need experience working in hotels.
3 ☐ Martin is free to work this summer.
4 ☐ Martin would like to learn some new skills.
5 ☐ Martin doesn't have any previous experience working in hotels.
6 ☐ Martin would like more details about the job.

2 WRITING SKILLS Organising an email

a Match 1–8 with a–h to make sentences.

1 [g] I'm writing to
2 ☐ I have five years'
3 ☐ I would like to work for your company
4 ☐ I have a lot of experience
5 ☐ My experience working in a busy hospital
6 ☐ I attach a copy of my CV with
7 ☐ Could you please send me information
8 ☐ I look forward to

a working in a team and dealing with customers.
b about the working hours and training programme?
c more information about my past employment.
d because it would be a good opportunity to learn some new skills.
e hearing from you.
f experience working as a secretary in a busy hospital.
g apply for the job of secretary.
h will be very useful for this job.

www.jobs-in-spain.com

Hotel Receptionist Wanted

We're looking for a hardworking and friendly receptionist to work in a hotel in Granada this summer. You will need to speak Spanish and at least one other language.

We prefer someone with experience working in hotels.

Accommodation and meals provided.

Apply online at www.casaalhambrahotel.com by 31st May.

Subject: Hotel Receptionist

Dear Sir/Madam,

I am writing to apply for the job of receptionist at the Casa Alhambra Hotel, which you advertised on jobs-in-spain.com.

I am studying French and Spanish at Bath University and am available to work in July and August.

I would like to work for you because it would be a good opportunity for me to learn new skills and to work in a team. I have worked in a hotel before as a waiter, so I have experience dealing with customers and working in a busy hotel environment.

I attach a copy of my CV with details of my previous experience.

Could you please send me information about the salary, the working hours and the accommodation?

I look forward to hearing from you.

Yours faithfully,

Martin Evans

3 WRITING

a Read the job advert and write an email applying for the job.

www.abc-jobs.co.uk

Sales Assistant Wanted

T-World are looking for a hard-working sales assistant to sell all types of computers, tablets, game consoles, smart TVs and smartphones in our brand-new superstore in Brighton.

We are offering a good salary plus sales bonus to the right person.

You will need previous sales experience and a good understanding of the latest technology.

We prefer someone with experience working in a busy environment.

Full training programme given.

Apply by 30th September to salesassistant@t-world.co.uk.

UNIT 5
Reading and listening extension

1 READING

a Read the article. Match the people 1–4 with pictures a–d.

1 ☐ Malcolm
2 ☐ Freya
3 ☐ Cara
4 ☐ James

a
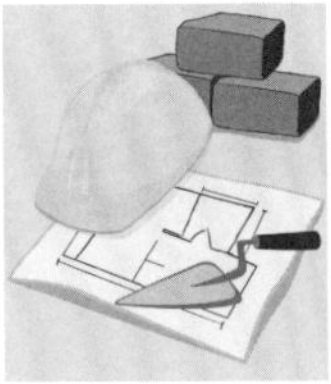
b

c
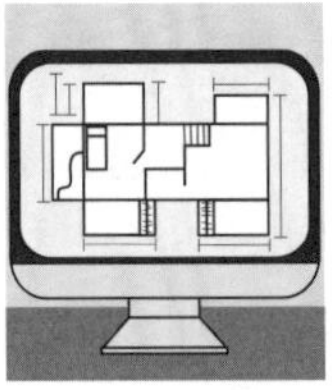
d

b Read the article again and tick (✓) the correct boxes. Sometimes there is more than one possible answer.

	Gets paid well	Works and studies	Is doing something they love	Has to work long hours every day
1 Malcolm		✓		
2 Freya				
3 Cara				
4 James				

c Read the article again and underline the correct answer. Sometimes there is more than one possible answer.

1 Who works for themselves?
a Malcolm b Freya c Cara d James
2 Who doesn't earn any money?
a Malcolm b Freya c Cara d James
3 Who has the weekends free?
a Malcolm b Freya c Cara d James
4 Who likes the place where they work?
a Malcolm b Freya c Cara d James
5 Who studies and works in a different place?
a Malcolm b Freya c Cara d James

d Write a paragraph about a job you'd like to do. Remember to include:

- the things you'd like to do in the job
- the hours
- the salary
- the environment.

Where to now?

When you finish school or university, you must think carefully about what you would like to do next. Here, some young people tell us their experiences.

I thought about my skills and qualifications and then about me. I've always liked working in a team, I like being outside and I decided I can't work in an office every day. Someone suggested I train to be a builder. I go to classes Monday and Friday and I work Tuesday to Thursday. I have to get up early so I can't go out in the evenings, but I'm learning a useful skill.

Malcolm, 19

I work for a number of companies as a book designer. I'm self-employed, which means I work on my own and not in a team. When I'm very busy, I have to work long hours, in the evenings and sometimes at weekends. But I really like my job and I can work at home, so I can say that I have a really nice working environment! I don't have to deal with customers or a manager! When I'm busy, I can earn a good salary, but I'm not always busy.

Cara, 28

I love art and design and I've always wanted to do something I enjoy. I decided to study to become an architect. I'm learning so much and I'm doing what I want, which is really important. I have to study every day of the week and I just hope I can find a job when I leave university.

Freya, 21

I've always liked animals. Earning a really good salary is important to me too, so I studied to be a vet. I have to work long hours and I have to study at home most weekends, but I know it is worth it when I'm helping sick animals.

James, 24

2 LISTENING

a 05.04 Listen to the conversation. What did Josh say about these jobs? Tick (✓) the correct boxes. Sometimes there is more than one possible answer.

	Builder	Hairdresser	IT worker	Bank clerk
1 Work long hours	✓			
2 Nice working environment				
3 Deal with people				
4 Earn a good salary				
5 Work in a team				

b 05.04 Listen to the conversation again and complete the table to show what Josh liked and disliked about the jobs. Write one word in each space.

	He liked …	He disliked …
1 Builder	working ___outside___.	starting work ________.
2 Hairdresser	learning new ________.	dealing with ________.
3 IT worker	________ work when he wanted.	working at ________.

c Choose one of the following:

1 Write a conversation between two people. Person A is interviewing Person B for the job of a journalist. Person B explains why he/she is the right person for the job and asks five questions about the job. Person A asks questions and answers the questions Person B asks.
2 Write about the parts of a job you would be happy to do and what you definitely wouldn't like to do.

Review and extension

1 GRAMMAR

Correct the sentences.

1 Tomorrow's Sunday, so I mustn't get up early.
Tomorrow's Sunday, so I don't have to get up early.
2 Excuse me, sir. You don't have to eat in the laboratory. It's against the rules.
3 Do you must wear a suit to work?
4 When I finish school, I can go to university. It depends on my grades.
5 I've to start work at 7 o'clock in the morning in my new job!
6 I'll take my umbrella. It can rain this afternoon.

2 VOCABULARY

Correct the sentences.

1 In your new job, I'm sure they'll give you a lot of trainings.
In your new job, I'm sure they'll give you a lot of training.
2 My sister works as a shop assistent in a big department store.
3 You need good qualification if you want to become a doctor.
4 He works as a disigner for a top fashion magazine.
5 If you want to become a plummer, you'll need to do a training programme.
6 My brother wants to become a professional music.

3 WORDPOWER *job* and *work*

Underline the correct words to complete the sentences.

1 The GPS on my phone doesn't *work* / *job* very well when I'm driving through the mountains.
2 I've found a really good *job* / *work* at the local newspaper.
3 No, I can't go to the cinema. I have to stay late at *job* / *work*.
4 My headache's a little better, so I think that medicine's beginning to *work* / *job*.
5 What time do you start *job* / *work* in the mornings?
6 He has to *work* / *job* all weekend on that report.
7 I'm studying for my final exams – it's really hard *job* / *work*.
8 My dad has a lot of small *jobs* / *works* to do in the garden.
9 My dad can't *work* / *job* out at the moment because he hurt his back last week.

REVIEW YOUR PROGRESS

Look again at Review Your Progress on p. 56 of the Student's Book. How well can you do these things now?
3 = very well 2 = well 1 = not so well

I CAN …	
talk about what people do at work	☐
talk about my future career	☐
make offers and suggestions	☐
write a job application.	☐

6A YOU SHOULD HAVE A BREAK

1 GRAMMAR Imperative; *should*

a Complete the text with the words in the box.

should go don't use eat should read shouldn't drink go don't sit should have shouldn't have ~~get~~

Here are some ideas for those of you who have problems sleeping:

First of all, 1 get plenty of exercise during the day. For example, 2 ____________ for a long walk at lunchtime or after work. 3 ____________ at home watching TV all evening. Secondly, you 4 ____________ dinner late in the evening. 5 ____________ dinner at least four hours before you go to bed. Also, you 6 ____________ coffee after 4 pm – it will stop you from sleeping. Next, 7 ____________ your laptop or your phone when you're in bed. Instead, you 8 ____________ a good book at bedtime – it's very relaxing. Also, some people find it hard to sleep if their room isn't dark enough, so you 9 ____________ thick curtains in your bedroom so that the light doesn't wake you up too early in the morning. Finally, you 10 ____________ to bed at the same time every night. Doing this tells your body that it's time for you to go to sleep. Sweet dreams, everyone!

b Correct the sentences. Use *should*, *shouldn't* or the imperative.

1 He shouldn't listening to music while he's studying.
He shouldn't listen to music while he's studying.

2 To eat a lot of fruit and vegetables every day.
____

3 Not use your computer for very long in the evenings.
____

4 You should to try to relax for an hour before you go to bed.
____

5 I think she should getting more exercise during the day.
____

6 You don't should go swimming immediately after lunch.
____

7 When you have a headache, to drink some water.
____

8 Don't stay you at work after six o'clock.
____

2 VOCABULARY Verbs with dependent prepositions

a Match 1–8 with a–h to make sentences.

1 [e] When you called me, I was looking
2 [ ] The train from Manchester arrived
3 [ ] Can you think
4 [ ] He was listening
5 [ ] Could you deal
6 [ ] He asked his father
7 [ ] Matthew decided to talk
8 [ ] My father wants to pay

a for £50 because he needed a new shirt for the wedding.
b to his son's teacher about his exam results.
c for lunch with his credit card.
d of a nice present for your grandfather's birthday?
e at an old photo of when we were in school.
f with this order for six takeaway pizzas, please?
g to the football match on the radio.
h at Euston Station 25 minutes late.

b Underline the correct words to complete the sentences.

1 In my job, I have to deal *about* / *for* / *with* customers all day long.
2 It's hard to concentrate *with* / *on* / *for* my homework when you're listening to the radio.
3 This bus is crowded! I'll wait *for* / *to* / *from* the next one.
4 His girlfriend's gone to Paris for a month, so he thinks *from* / *about* / *for* her all the time.
5 They don't pay you much do they? You should ask your boss *from* / *on* / *for* a pay rise.
6 Jackie says she spends about £200 a month *at* / *on* / *to* clothes!
7 If you want to buy a new car now, you should borrow some money *with* / *for* / *from* the bank.
8 He's really generous. He paid *with* / *for* / *of* my plane ticket to New York!

3 PRONUNCIATION Sound and spelling: /uː/ and /ʊ/

a 06.01 Listen to the sentences. Are the vowel sounds in **bold** long /uː/ or short /ʊ/? Tick (✓) the correct box for each sentence.

	long /uː/	short /ʊ/
1 We t**oo**k my grandmother to the theatre.		✓
2 The children wanted to go to the z**oo**.		
3 Where did you l**o**se your mobile phone?		
4 W**ou**ld you like a cup of coffee?		
5 Wh**o** did you invite to the party?		
6 I don't think you sh**ou**ld go to work today.		
7 C**ou**ld I borrow £5, please?		
8 What did you think of the f**oo**d?		

6B I WAS VERY FRIGHTENED

1 VOCABULARY *-ed / -ing* adjectives

a Underline the correct words to complete the sentences.

1 I thought the Tokyo Metro was really *confused* / *confusing*. There are too many metro lines!
2 The football match was very *exciting* / *excited*. It finished 4 – 4.
3 Tracy isn't very *interesting* / *interested* in video games.
4 I was *shocked* / *shocking* when I saw him. He looked very ill.
5 She was very *annoyed* / *annoying* when he asked her for some more money.
6 The flight from London to Mexico City was very *tired* / *tiring*.
7 I thought the view from the top of the Eiffel Tower was *amazing* / *amazed*.
8 He felt *embarrassing* / *embarrassed* when his mum kissed him in front of his friends.

b Complete the sentences with adjectives ending in *-ed* or *-ing*.

1 The people in the flat above me are so annoying. They play loud music when I'm trying to go to sleep.
2 He looked really c__________ when he woke up. He said, 'Where am I?'
3 I thought that documentary about Martin Luther King Jr. was really i__________.
4 The exam results were very s__________. Nobody got higher than 50%!
5 She was very f__________ when she saw the spider, but she calmed down when we told her it was plastic.
6 He was very d__________ that his father didn't bring him a present from Spain.
7 They couldn't speak a word when they heard the s__________ news that the singer was dead.
8 She felt very e__________ when he told her that they were going on holiday to Florida.

2 GRAMMAR Uses of *to* + infinitive

a Put the words in the correct order to make sentences.

1 job / I / to / disappointed / get / not / was / the .
I was disappointed not to get the job.
2 sharks / was / learn / interesting / it / to / about .
____
3 our cars / you / tell us / park / where / can / to ?
____
4 wear / is / not / dangerous / to / a seat belt / it .
____
5 her / relax / to / she / a bath / help / had .
____
6 the bus station / went / to / meet / aunt / to / they / their .
____
7 her father / she / him / to / some money / ask / for / called .
____
8 didn't / he / what / to the party / know / wear / to .
____

b Correct the sentences.

1 They wanted buy him a nice birthday present.
They wanted to buy him a nice birthday present.
2 He asked me how getting to the airport.
____
3 She was annoyed to not receive an invitation to his wedding.
____
4 They went to the supermarket for buy some food for dinner.
____
5 We couldn't remember which bus catching to the airport.
____
6 John and Angela decided to have not their wedding in Ireland.
____
7 It was embarrassing fail my driving test again.
____
8 She went to the library for borrow a book about dinosaurs for her son.
____

6C EVERYDAY ENGLISH

What do you think I should do?

1 USEFUL LANGUAGE Asking for and giving advice; Showing sympathy

a Match sentences 1–8 with responses a–h.

1 [d] I think it's a good idea to book a table. The restaurant might be full.
2 [ ] Someone stole my handbag when I was at the beach this afternoon.
3 [ ] I'd speak to your boss about it.
4 [ ] I wouldn't worry too much. You can get a new passport at the embassy.
5 [ ] Do you think I should invite Steve to the surprise party?
6 [ ] What do you think I should do?
7 [ ] I didn't get the job in marketing.
8 [ ] I broke my finger on Saturday.

a Oh, what a pity. I'm sure you'll get another job soon.
b Oh, that's a shame. So that means you can't play tennis today?
c No, I don't think that's a very good idea. Anna doesn't like him very much.
d Yes, I suppose so. Saturday night can be very busy.
e How awful! I'm really sorry to hear that.
f I don't think I should do that. She'll be angry with me.
g Yes, you're right. I can go there one day next week.
h I think you should go to the police station.

b 06.02 Listen and check.

c Put the words in the correct order to make sentences.

1 apply for / which / should / do / job / you / I / think ?
Which job do you think I should apply for?
2 colleagues / should / I / your / you / think / ask .
______
3 sorry / really / that / hear / to / I'm .
______
4 new job / a / should / do / think / I / you / look / for ?
______
5 I / a / think it's / to / your boss / speak / to / good idea .
______
6 about / talk / I'd / your parents / it / to .
______
7 apply / I / for / marketing job / new / the / wouldn't .
______
8 think / I / you / your / don't / job / leave / should .
______

d 06.03 Listen and check.

2 PRONUNCIATION Main stress

a 06.04 Listen to the sentences and tick (✓) the stressed words.

1 You're from Canada, right?
a [ ] You're b [✓] Canada
2 Elena works in the Spanish Embassy.
a [ ] Spanish b [ ] Embassy
3 Would you like to work in London?
a [ ] work b [ ] London
4 We're having a surprise party for Anna.
a [ ] party b [ ] Anna
5 My boss wants to speak to me.
a [ ] boss b [ ] me

6D SKILLS FOR WRITING

I often worry about tests and exams

1 READING

a Read Anthony's email to Marina and Marina's reply. Tick (✓) the correct answer.

a ☐ Anthony is looking for a new job.
b ☐ Anthony doesn't want Jim to leave his job.
c ☐ Marina gives Anthony some ideas to help him.
d ☐ Marina works as a manager in a bank in Seville.

Dear Marina,

The problem is that I'm feeling very stressed about my job at the moment. You see, Jim, one of the people on my team, has just left. They haven't replaced Jim yet, so my boss has given all of his work to the other people in the team, including me. Do you have any advice for me?

Sincerely,

Anthony

Dear Anthony,

Thank you for your email. I'm very pleased that you have written to me for advice.

This kind of situation is very common in companies when somebody leaves. I remember this happened when I was working in a bank in Seville. One summer, two of the people in my team left the bank at the same time. We had to do all of their work and it took three months to replace them! Anyway, here are some ideas that might help you.

First of all, try not to get too stressed about the situation. I think you should discuss the problem with your colleagues. Maybe they will have some ideas about how to make the situation a bit easier? Secondly, when you've got too much work to do, I think it's a good idea to try to prioritise your work carefully. For example, are there some less urgent jobs that you could do later?

Next, I think you should talk to your boss about this problem. He might not realise how much work he has given you, and maybe he can find some other people to help you with it. Finally, I'd try to do something relaxing after work, such as going to the gym or going swimming. It's important to relax when you aren't at work and to get plenty of sleep.

I hope this helps you and please feel free to come and talk to me in my office.

Best wishes,

Marina Rodriguez

HR Manager

b Read the emails again. Are the sentences true (*T*) or false (*F*)?

1 ☐ Anthony is doing all of Jim's work.
2 ☐ Marina was the manager of a team of two people at the bank.
3 ☐ Marina thinks that Anthony should talk to his colleagues about the problem.
4 ☐ Marina doesn't think Anthony should discuss the problem with his manager.
5 ☐ Marina thinks it's a good idea for Anthony to relax after work.

2 WRITING SKILLS Linking: ordering ideas and giving examples

a Put *for example* or *such as* in the correct place in each sentence. Add capital letters and punctuation (. , ') and make any other necessary changes.

1 There are lots of ways to make new friends joining a sports club.
There are lots of ways to make new friends, such as joining a sports club.

2 It's a good idea to read something in English every day. You can read different newspapers online.
____

3 Why don't you do something relaxing this evening going for a swim after work?
____

4 There are more enjoyable ways of preparing for an exam. You could study with a friend who's in the same class.
____

5 You could start a new hobby to help you relax dancing or swimming.
____

3 WRITING

a Read Kento's message to his English teacher, Tina. Use the notes below to write Tina's reply.

Dear Tina,

I think I'm quite good at reading and writing in English, but listening is very hard for me. I really want to improve my listening. Do you have any ideas?

Thank you,

Kento

Notes for message to Kento:
Paragraph 1: say thanks
Paragraph 2: me: learning Japanese – listening v. difficult – explain why – ideas to help …
Paragraph 3:
1) impossible to understand every word – concentrate on most important words
2) extra practice – study centre – listening exercises, e.g. listening tracks from Student's Book
3) radio / TV in English, films (+ subtitles)
4) podcasts – short stories?
5) pop songs + read words – find websites
Paragraph 4: hope this helps – talk to me after class?

UNIT 6
Reading and listening extension

1 READING

a Read the magazine article and <u>underline</u> the correct people to match the adjectives.

1 annoyed	*Jade / <u>manager</u> / Eva*
2 embarrassed	*Jade / customers / Eva*
3 confused	*manager / Eva / Jade*
4 frightened	*Jade / manager / customers*
5 not disappointed	*customers / Jade / Eva*
6 surprised	*Jade / customers / Eva*

b Read the magazine article again. Tick (✓) the correct answers.

1 What is Jade's problem?
- a ☐ She doesn't like spending time with customers.
- b ☑ Her manager thinks she works too slowly.
- c ☐ She gets confused by what the customers say to her.

2 Who is Toni?
- a ☐ one of Jade's customers
- b ☐ Jade's manager
- c ☐ another hairdresser

3 When does Jade get embarrassed?
- a ☐ when her manager gets angry with her in front of customers
- b ☐ when the customers talk to her
- c ☐ when her manager looks at her

4 What surprises Eva?
- a ☐ Toni talks to Jade in front of customers.
- b ☐ Toni doesn't understand the customers.
- c ☐ Toni doesn't understand what good customer service is.

5 What advice does Eva give?
- a ☐ She thinks Jade should tell her manager how she feels.
- b ☐ She tells Jade not to think about it.
- c ☐ She thinks that Jade's customers should talk to Toni.

c Read the magazine article again. Match 1–5 with a–e to make sentences.

1 [*c*] Jade thinks that a customer who
2 [ ] Toni thinks that Jade
3 [ ] Jade can't concentrate when Toni
4 [ ] Jade is confused because she
5 [ ] Eva thinks that Toni

a keeps looking at her.
b shouldn't spend so much time talking to customers.
c spends a lot of money should get good service.
d thinks she is very good at her job.
e will change his mind after the customers talk to him.

d Write an email to Jade giving her some advice about her problem. Remember to include:

- some advice
- some instructions
- a similar situation from your own life.

Ask — Eva —

Every week, our experts answer your problems. This week, Eva Perez, our writer and management expert, answers a question about a problem at work.

Dear Eva,

I need to ask you for some help.

I'm a hairdresser and I work in a very fashionable salon. I'm very good at dealing with the customers and I like to talk to them when I cut their hair. They pay a lot of money for their haircuts, and I think it's important to spend time with them and make sure they're happy. But my manager, a man named Toni, gets really annoyed with me and keeps telling me to work faster. He sometimes talks to me in front of the customers, which makes me really embarrassed. He looks at me all the time when I talk to them and now I find it really difficult to concentrate on what I'm doing.

I'm really confused. I'm a really good hairdresser. None of the customers are ever disappointed with my work and I get on well with all my colleagues. I'm frightened of losing my job if I say anything.

Can you help me?

Jade

Dear Jade,

You're right. When customers spend a lot of money on a haircut, they should enjoy the experience, feel relaxed and get excellent service. I'm surprised Toni doesn't understand this. How many of your customers would come back if you spent less than 15 minutes with them?

I think you should ask your customers for help. Ask them to talk to or write an email to your manager telling him what they like about the service you give them. I think your manager will soon change his mind.

Good luck!

Eva

2 LISTENING

a 06.05 Listen to three friends talking about studying. Tick (✓) the people that match the statements.

	Ellie	Maya	Owen
1 I can't study at home.	✓		
2 I study in the library.			
3 I haven't got a good memory.			
4 I listen to a recording of myself to help me remember.			
5 I can help someone with their revision.			

b 06.05 Listen to the three friends talk about studying again. Tick (✓) the correct answers.

1 What is Ellie's problem?
 a ☑ Her brother is disturbing her.
 b ☐ She hasn't got a laptop to use for studying.
 c ☐ She doesn't want to go to the library to study.

2 What does Owen suggest Ellie do?
 a ☐ She should go to the library to study.
 b ☐ She must tell someone to stop.
 c ☐ She should ask her parents to help her with the problem.

3 What is Ellie going to do?
 a ☐ Talk to someone about the problem.
 b ☐ Go somewhere else to avoid the problem.
 c ☐ Talk to someone and go somewhere else.

4 Who has a problem with history?
 a ☐ Ellie
 b ☐ Owen
 c ☐ Maya

5 What is Ellie embarrassed about?
 a ☐ Her poor memory.
 b ☐ Making a song to help her study.
 c ☐ Her marks in the physics exam.

6 What is Maya's problem?
 a ☐ She is confused by a subject.
 b ☐ She doesn't want to study a subject.
 c ☐ She has to take a subject again next year.

c Write to somebody giving advice about how he or she can get better exam results.

Review and extension

1 GRAMMAR

Correct the sentences.

1 You shouldn't to drink coffee before you go to bed.
 You shouldn't drink coffee before you go to bed.
2 I think he should doing some exercise every day.
3 You should read a book for to help you relax.
4 She asked me drive her to the station.
5 My father taught me how play the guitar.
6 What I should do if I can't sleep well?

2 VOCABULARY

Correct the sentences.

1 The football match was really excited. It finished 3 – 3.
 The football match was really exciting. It finished 3 – 3.
2 I was thinking in that TV programme I saw last night.
3 My uncle paid the tickets and bought popcorn for us as well.
4 I can't afford to spend a lot of money in a holiday this year.
5 My little sister isn't very interesting in fashion.
6 I didn't hear the phone because I was listening some music.
7 I didn't think that horror film was frightened. What about you?
8 I didn't have any money, so I had to borrow £20 to my brother.

3 WORDPOWER Verb + *to*

Complete the sentences with the words in the box.

read sold paid wrote lent described ~~explained~~ brought

1 She *explained* the problem to her parents.
2 I ________ £200 to Jack so he could buy a phone.
3 He ________ a lot of food to the party.
4 Gianni ________ an email to the school asking for information about their language classes.
5 We ________ £500 to the builder who fixed our roof.
6 She ________ the story very quietly to her class, closed the book and put it back on the shelf.
7 They ________ their car to their neighbour for £1,500.
8 Laura ________ her new house in Australia to me.

REVIEW YOUR PROGRESS

Look again at Review Your Progress on p. 66 of the Student's Book. How well can you do these things now?
3 = very well 2 = well 1 = not so well

I CAN ...	
give advice for common problems	☐
describe extreme experiences	☐
ask for and give advice	☐
write an email giving advice.	☐

7A I'M THE HAPPIEST I'VE EVER BEEN

1 GRAMMAR
Comparatives and superlatives

a Read the information in the table about London, New York and Buenos Aires. Complete the sentences with the correct forms of the adjectives in brackets.

	London	New York	Buenos Aires
Average max. daily temperature: January	8°C	3°C	29°C
Average max. daily temperature: July	23°C	29°C	15°C
Population	8.9 million	8.6 million	2.8 million
Size	1,500 km²	1,200 km²	203 km²
Average hotel price	$167	$247	$64

1 In July, London isn't as __warm__ as New York. (warm)
2 Buenos Aires is the ________ city in January. (hot)
3 New York is ________ than London in January. (cold)
4 Buenos Aires is less ________ than New York in January. (cold)
5 Buenos Aires has the ________ population. (small)
6 Buenos Aires isn't as ________ as London. (big)
7 London is ________ than New York. (large)
8 Hotels in New York are ________ than hotels in Buenos Aires. (expensive)

b Put the words in the correct order to make sentences.

1 job / as / isn't / new / my old one / interesting / my / as .
My new job isn't as interesting as my old one.
2 film / it's / the / seen / exciting / ever / I've / most / I think .
____
3 happier / is / ever / she's / than / my sister / been .
____
4 to understand her / more / she speaks / quickly / because / you / it's hard / than .
____
5 one of / best / he / the USA / universities / to / in / went / the .
____
6 was / much warmer / the weather's / yesterday / it / than .
____
7 her sister / than / she / got / and / worked / in her exam / 95% / harder .
____
8 a year ago / English / speaks / than / much better / now / he .
____

2 VOCABULARY *get* collocations

a Underline the correct words to complete the sentences.

1 I *get together* / *get to know* / *get on well with* both of my sisters – we're very close.
2 I'm going to Australia on business next week, so I'll *get married* / *get in touch with* / *get to know* my friend Chris, who lives in Sydney.
3 In 2003, he married a Japanese woman and decided to stay in Japan because he *got a place at* / *got work* / *got an offer* as a language teacher in Tokyo.
4 When she went to live in Cambridge, she *got to know* / *got better* / *got engaged* her neighbours very quickly because everyone was so friendly.
5 Annie and Luis *got better* / *got divorced* / *got together* after they met at a friend's birthday two years ago. It was love at first sight.
6 If you don't drink bottled water, you might *get ill* / *get better* / *get old* because the water isn't very clean here.
7 In my company, we normally *get rich* / *get paid* / *get an offer* on the last day of the month.
8 My parents *got married* / *got divorced* / *got engaged* last year, but they are still good friends.

b Complete the sentences with the correct forms of the expressions in the box.

get engaged   get rich   ~~get better~~   get paid
get to know   get a place   get an offer   get married

1 Josh broke his leg playing football last year. Luckily, he __got better__ very quickly and he's going skiing next month!
2 My parents ________ in 1995 and I was born in 1998.
3 He bought her a beautiful silver ring when they ________ last month.
4 You might ________ at Harvard University if you study very hard and do really well in your exams.
5 He ________ when he sold his software company to Google five years ago.
6 Emma was working as a model in Paris when she ________ to be in a French film.
7 We ________ a lot of really interesting people when we lived in Dublin.
8 Brad Pitt ________ over $20 million for his last film.

7B I DIDN'T USE TO EAT HEALTHY FOOD

1 VOCABULARY Health collocations

a Match 1–8 with a–h to make sentences.

1 [c] She gave up
2 [ ] I've lost a lot of
3 [ ] I'm sure he's put on
4 [ ] My plan is to get
5 [ ] A lot of people today don't keep
6 [ ] She keeps fit
7 [ ] It's important to have a healthy
8 [ ] I was a regular

a by exercising regularly and eating healthily.
b fit by going to the gym twice a week starting in January.
c fast food three years ago and now feels much healthier.
d in shape because they don't get enough exercise.
e smoker for ten years, but now I've stopped.
f weight since I started a new fitness programme.
g weight because he doesn't look as thin as he did last year.
h diet with plenty of vegetables and fruit.

b Complete the sentences with the words in the box.

get gave up ~~keeps~~ stress put on
allergies smoker lack of healthy

1 She _keeps_ fit by going to the gym twice a week and running.
2 He ___________ a lot of weight a year ago. Now he's on a ___________ diet and he looks fitter.
3 She suffered from ___________ after working 12 hours a day for six months.
4 If you go swimming three times a week, you'll ___________ fit very quickly.
5 My uncle sleeps better because he ___________ drinking coffee last month.
6 Last winter he suffered from a ___________ Vitamin D because he spent little time in the sun.
7 Do you have any ___________ to certain types of food, such as seafood or peanuts?
8 She was a regular ___________ for a long time, but she suddenly decided to stop last year.

2 GRAMMAR *used to*

a Rewrite the highlighted phrases. Use the correct forms of *used to*.

Twenty years ago, when I was a student, I use to live [1] _I used to live_ in a large house with five of my friends. We usedn't to have [2] ___________ much money, so we didn't used to go [3] ___________ out to restaurants or clubs in the evenings.

Instead, we use to invite [4] ___________ our friends to come to our house in the evenings. One of my friends, Sandro, was Italian, and he use to cook [5] ___________ fantastic meals for us, such as pizza or pasta. After dinner, we used watch [6] ___________ TV or listen to music together.

Another friend of mine, Jordi, used play [7] ___________ the guitar and teach us beautiful Spanish folk songs. Fortunately, our neighbours not used to complain [8] ___________ about the noise we made.

What about you? Used you to live [9] ___________ with a group of friends when you were at university, or you used to live [10] ___________ with your family?

b Complete the sentences with the correct forms of *used to* and the verbs in brackets.

1 We _used to have_ a dog, but it died five years ago. (have)
2 Molly ___________ bread from the supermarket, but now she has to get it there because her favourite bakery closed last month. (buy)
3 What ___________ you ___________ for lunch when you were in school? (eat)
4 She ___________ German quite well, but she hasn't spoken it for ten years so she's forgotten most of it. (speak)
5 I ___________ the bus to work every day, but now I usually cycle or walk. (take)
6 ___________ you ___________ with dolls when you were little? (play)
7 My grandfather ___________ a computer, but he's got one now. (have)
8 We ___________ black-and-white films at the cinema when I was young. We thought they were brilliant! (watch)

7C EVERYDAY ENGLISH
It hurts all the time

1 USEFUL LANGUAGE
Describing symptoms; Doctors' questions

a Match the doctor's sentences 1–8 with the patient's responses a–h.

1 [d] So, what's the problem?
2 [ ] When did this start?
3 [ ] Where does it hurt? Can you show me?
4 [ ] Can I have a look? So, does it hurt here?
5 [ ] Are you taking anything for the pain?
6 [ ] Well, I don't think it's anything to worry about.
7 [ ] I think it's just indigestion.
8 [ ] I'll give you a prescription for some medicine. Take two pills every four hours.

a Just indigestion? What a relief!
b OK. Thank you, Doctor.
c Phew! That's good to hear.
d I've got a stomach ache. It's really painful.
e Yes, it does. It hurts all the time. I can't get to sleep.
f Yes, I've taken some paracetamol.
g About two days ago.
h Here, in this area.

b 07.01 Listen and check.

c Complete the sentences with the words in the box.

relief taking ~~worry~~ you'll problem hear
~~nothing~~ sick hurts look shouldn't get

1 Don't _worry_. It's _nothing_ to worry about.
2 Phew! That's good to ________.
3 It ________ all the time. I can't ________ to sleep.
4 Can I have a ________?
5 Are you ________ anything for the pain?
6 I feel ________ and exhausted.
7 I think ________ need to see another doctor.
8 So, what's the ________?
9 What a ________!
10 You ________ stay in bed.

d 07.02 Listen and check.

e Put the conversation in the correct order.

[ ] Yes! Very much. Is it broken?
[ ] OK, Doctor. Thank you.
[ ] Can you show me where it hurts?
[1] So, what brings you here today?
[ ] Does it hurt if I touch it here?
[ ] Right here, next to my wrist.
[ ] I've hurt my arm. I fell off my bike.
[ ] No, I don't think so. I'll put a bandage on it.

2 PRONUNCIATION
Intonation for asking questions

a 07.03 Listen to the questions. Tick (✓) to show if the doctor's voice goes up ↗ or down ↘ at the end.

		↗	↘
1	Do you do any exercise?	✓	
2	When did this problem start?		
3	Could you have a few tests tomorrow?		
4	How many pills have you taken?		
5	How long have you had this problem?		
6	Are you taking anything for the pain?		
7	Do you have any allergies?		
8	Have you had any accidents recently?		

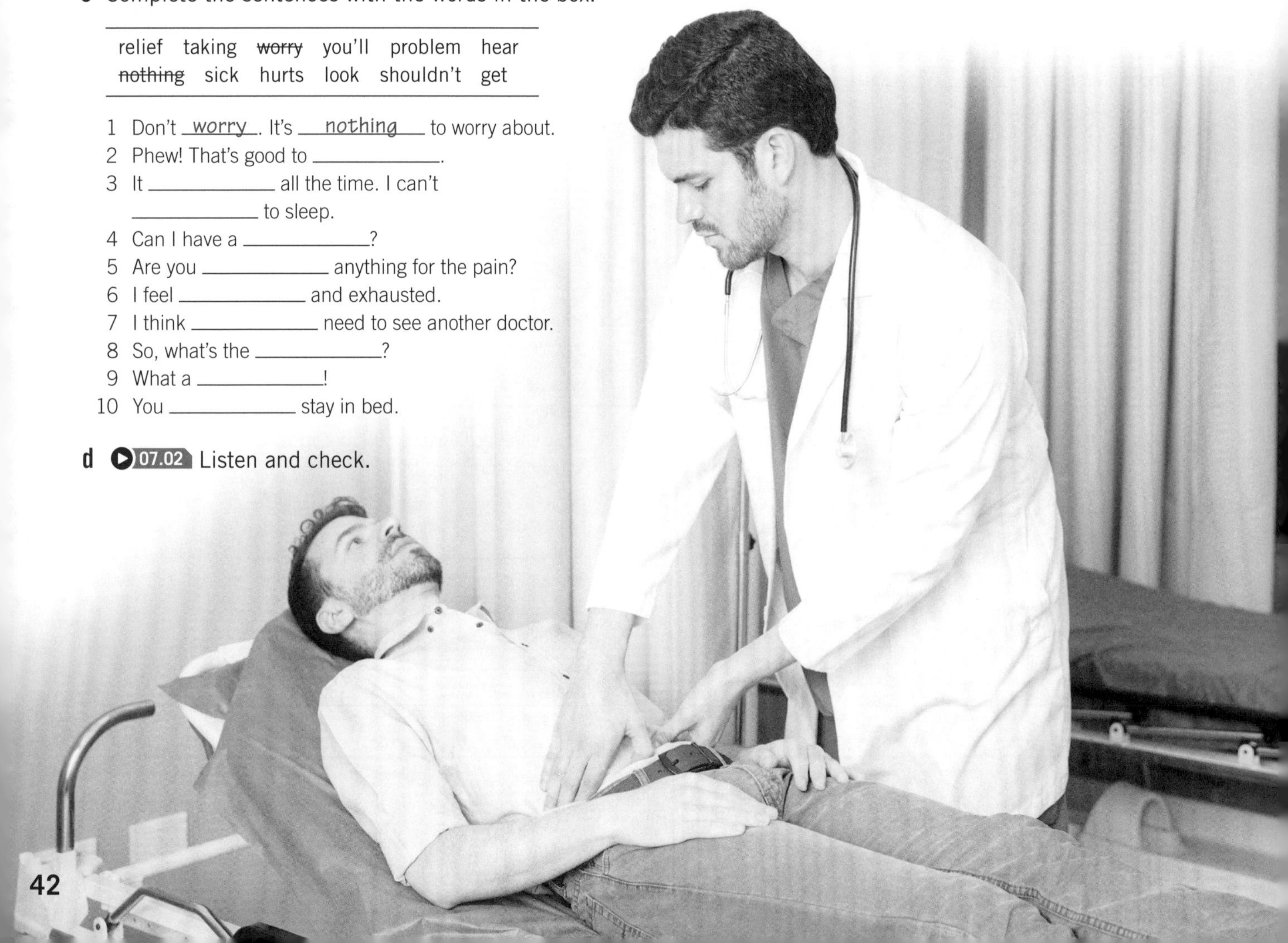

7D SKILLS FOR WRITING
After that, I decided to make a change

1 READING

a Read Nicola's blog on the right and tick (✓) the correct answer.

a ☐ Nicola could speak Spanish very well two years ago.
b ☐ Nicola lives and works in Madrid.
c ☐ Nicola wanted to get a new job as a manager.
d ☐ Nicola studied Spanish at university.

b Read the blog again. Are the sentences true (*T*) or false (*F*)?

1 ☐ Two years ago, Nicola didn't get on well with her colleagues in the bank.
2 ☐ Managers in Nicola's bank need to have a very good level of Spanish.
3 ☐ Nicola used to buy a Spanish newspaper every day.
4 ☐ Nicola studied Spanish at a language school in Madrid.
5 ☐ Nicola is going to work for her bank in their Madrid office.

HOME | ABOUT | BLOG

NICOLA123

About two years ago, my job was getting really boring. I liked the bank and enjoyed working with my colleagues, but I needed a change. I wanted to become a manager because I thought the work would be more interesting and that I would have the chance to travel to different countries.

However, I knew that it was very important for managers in my bank to write and speak excellent Spanish. I studied Spanish at school, but I stopped when I was 16, so I couldn't remember much. I decided to try and improve my Spanish quickly so that I could apply for a job as a manager.

To begin with, I studied my old Spanish textbook from school and did a lot of exercises. After that, I started reading Spanish newspapers online for 30 minutes every day and looked up the meaning of any new words in my dictionary. Soon I could understand nearly everything I read. After a while, I found a website where I could practise listening and speaking. Then I joined a Spanish class at a language school in my town and went to classes twice a week. In the end, after about 18 months, I could understand and speak Spanish well.

I decided to start applying for management jobs at the bank, and last month I got an offer for a job in Madrid. My new job starts in September, so I have a few weeks to find a flat. I'm really excited about going to live in Madrid.

2 WRITING SKILLS
Linking: ordering events

a Complete the blog below with the words in the box.

then	the end	after	soon	a while	~~first~~

How I became **a top chef**

Three years ago, I was a terrible cook. I could cook some eggs for my family, but I couldn't cook anything more exciting than that. Two years later, I got a job in a top London restaurant as a chef. Shall I tell you how I did it?

At [1] *first*, my wife helped me. She showed me how to make some simple dishes, such as roast chicken and potatoes and spaghetti bolognese. [2] ________ that, I started going to cooking classes at a college in London, where I learned how to cook a lot of different dishes from all over the world. [3] ________ I started inviting my friends to my house for dinner and I cooked some of the meals I had learnt at college. After [4] ________, my friends told me I was an amazing cook and that I should become a chef. [5] ________, I entered an important cooking competition on television and, to my surprise, I won! In [6] ________, I got an offer to work at the Ritz Hotel as one of their chefs, so I gave up my office job and I've never regretted it for one moment.

3 WRITING

a Read the notes and write Sophia's blog about how she changed her journey to work.

Notes for Sophia's blog

2 years ago: go to work by bus = a lot of traffic, 1 hour +
buy a bicycle? but not very fit

bought old bicycle from friend …
1) frightened of cycling on road – so many cars & lorries
2) went to a park – cycled slowly, 5–10 mins.
3) house to local shops – 2 km
4) house to city centre – 5 km
5) everywhere on my bike

now: 8 km to work – feel fit & healthy
only 30 mins to work – save 1 hour a day

UNIT 7
Reading and listening extension

Remembering the Past

As she celebrates her 100th birthday, Kimi Tanaka talks to *Youth2day* magazine about growing up.

1
My family didn't have much money, but my brothers and I had what we needed. We didn't feel poor. We were like everyone else around here. We used to get together with the other children and play outside every day. We all got on well. It was a nice place to be. Everything used to happen in that street. I met my future husband in the neighbourhood. He lived opposite us. When we got engaged, we had a party in the street. It was wonderful. It's changed a lot. It's a lot quieter now. The children don't play outside. I know their lives are busier, but I don't think the kids are happier. And they aren't as fit as we were! I can't believe that so many children spend hours looking at computer screens these days.

2
We used to eat three times a day and no more. We had a much healthier diet: a lot of vegetables, some meat and very little sugar. There didn't use to be fast food like crisps and burgers and no one needed to go to a gym to get fit. Everyone on our street, children and adults, used to work so hard.

3
It wasn't all better. A lot of people smoked. We didn't know how bad smoking was. My husband was a regular smoker. Fortunately, he gave up smoking when our children were born.

4
My husband used to work in the local car factory. He worked hard but didn't get paid very much. It was difficult sometimes. People are richer and their lives are easier now, especially with the Internet. But our lives were happier then. I wouldn't change my life then for anything.

1 READING

a Read the magazine article. Match the numbered paragraphs 1–4 with the titles a–d.

1 Paragraph 1 — c	a How We Used to Eat
2 Paragraph 2	b Not All About the Money
3 Paragraph 3	c Playing Outside
4 Paragraph 4	d Unknown Dangers

b Read the magazine article again and <u>underline</u> the correct answers.

Kimi thinks …

1 the streets <u>*are*</u> / *used to be* much quieter <u>*now*</u> / *in the past.*
2 the children *are* / *used to be* happier *now* / *in the past.*
3 people *have* / *used to have* healthier diets *now* / *in the past.*
4 more people *smoke* / *used to smoke* *now* / *in the past.*
5 people *are* / *used to be* richer *now* / *in the past.*

c Read the magazine article again and tick (✓) the correct answers.

1 Kimi's family …
   a ☐ were very poor.
   b ☐ had better lives than their neighbours.
   c ☑ were similar to the other families where they lived.

2 There was a party in the street …
   a ☐ before Kimi got married.
   b ☐ when Kimi got married.
   c ☐ when Kimi met her husband.

3 People didn't use to go to a gym to get fit because …
   a ☐ they didn't like doing exercise.
   b ☐ they preferred to eat fast food.
   c ☐ they worked so much.

4 People used to smoke a lot because …
   a ☐ it was much cheaper.
   b ☐ they didn't understand it was dangerous.
   c ☐ you could smoke and buy cigarettes everywhere.

5 Kimi thinks …
   a ☐ richer people are happier.
   b ☐ she would prefer to grow up now.
   c ☐ the Internet has made people's lives easier.

d Write about how your life has changed over the past ten years. Write about what you used to do and what you do now. Write about:

- your education
- your free time
- your friends and family.

2 LISTENING

a 07.04 Listen to the conversation. Complete the table with the names in the box.

Dale George   Lisa Baker   Martin Dowd
~~Mike Andrews~~   Steven Downes

	Name	20 years ago	Now
1	Mike Andrews	quiet	rich
2		popular	popular
3		friendly	serious
4		didn't like someone	is married to the person he didn't like
5		didn't like sport	fit and healthy

b 07.04 Listen to the conversation again and complete the sentences. Write one word in each space.

1 Steven Downes used to be married to Jenny Robertson.
2 Jenny wanted Steven to stop ________ and ________ coffee.
3 Lisa Baker has been on a ________ programme and is a lot ________ than she used to be.
4 Lisa is going to open her own ________ next month.
5 Mike Andrews is a lot ________ than he used to be.
6 Dale George didn't use to ________ Nicola Walker.

c Write about your friends and family ten years ago. Remember to include:

- what they used to do
- what they used to look like
- what they used to be like.

Review and extension

1 GRAMMAR

Correct the sentences.

1 Ronaldo is one of most famous footballers in the world.
Ronaldo is one of the most famous footballers in the world.
2 I think São Paulo is the most biggest city in Brazil.
3 My brother didn't used to like coffee when he was a teenager.
4 This exercise is more easier than the last one.
5 I'm studying harder this year as last year.
6 Sydney is the expensivest city in Australia.

2 VOCABULARY

Correct the sentences.

1 I think you should give out smoking if you want to get fit.
I think you should give up smoking if you want to get fit.
2 You'll have to do exercise every day if you want to keep up shape.
3 My brother has got a new job and gets paying very well.
4 She loves her boyfriend and I think they'll get engage soon.
5 While he was at university, he got to knowing Percem.

3 WORDPOWER *change*

Match 1–7 with a–g to make sentences.

1 [f] The waiter hasn't given you
2 [ ] OK, let's go and play tennis. You can change
3 [ ] When you go away on holiday, it's better to change
4 [ ] We always go to Spain. Let's go to Turkey
5 [ ] You should keep
6 [ ] To fly from London to Sydney, you usually have to
7 [ ] She planned to take the train to Edinburgh, but at the last minute she changed

a some change in your pocket for the bus.
b this summer for a change.
c your money at a bank, not at the airport.
d her mind and flew instead.
e change planes in Bangkok or Dubai.
f the right change. You gave him £20, not £10.
g into your shorts and trainers in the bathroom.

REVIEW YOUR PROGRESS

Look again at Review Your Progress on p. 76 of the Student's Book. How well can you do these things now?
3 = very well   2 = well   1 = not so well

I CAN ...	
talk about life-changing events	☐
describe health and lifestyle changes	☐
talk to the doctor	☐
write a blog about an achievement.	☐

8A THE PHOTO WAS TAKEN 90 YEARS AGO

1 VOCABULARY Art, music and literature

a Look at the types of art, music and literature and label the pictures.

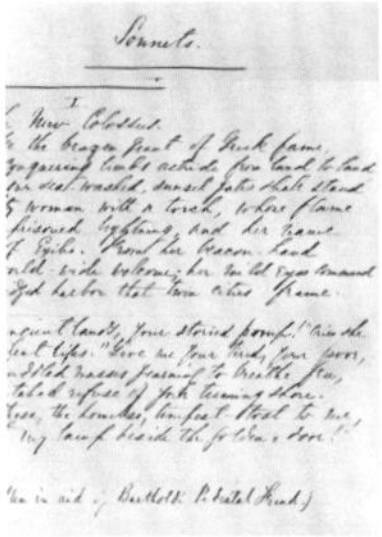

1 poem

2 ________

3 ________

4 ________

5 ________

6 ________

7 ________

8 ________

b Read the sentences. Which topic is each person talking about, architecture (A), music (M) or literature (L)?

1 [M] 'At the age of five, he was already composing songs.'
2 [ ] 'The best-selling album was recorded in one week.'
3 [ ] 'The novel was translated into more than 20 languages.'
4 [ ] 'The Guggenheim Museum is known for its unusual design.'
5 [ ] 'Two hundred years later, her poetry is still studied in schools.'
6 [ ] 'The pyramids in Central America were built by the Maya.'

2 GRAMMAR The passive: present simple and past simple

a Complete the sentences about the Statue of Liberty. Use the present or past simple passive forms of the verbs in brackets.

The Statue of Liberty [1] is known (know) around the world as a symbol of the United States, but it [2] ________ (not make) there. It [3] ________ (design) in France by Frédéric Auguste Bartholdi. It [4] ________ (give) to the USA by the people of France. The statue's head and arm [5] ________ (finish) first. In fact, these parts [6] ________ (make) before the rest of the statue [7] ________ (design). At first, there wasn't enough money to finish the rest of the statue. Finally, enough money [8] ________ (find). Over 120,000 people helped pay for the statue – most of them gave less than $1. The rest of the statue [9] ________ (create) in small pieces in France and the pieces [10] ________ (take) to the United States by ship. Finally, the statue [11] ________ (put) together in New York. It [12] ________ (finish) in 1886.These days, it [13] ________ (visit) by over 3.2 million tourists every year.

b Rewrite the sentences. Use the passive. Say who does/did the action only if this information is important.

1 They make Porsche cars in Germany.
Porsche cars are made in Germany.
2 They built the Eiffel Tower in 1889.
____
3 George Orwell wrote the novel *Nineteen Eighty-Four* in 1948.
____
4 They held the 2012 Olympic Games in London.
____
5 Steven Spielberg directed the film *Schindler's List* in 1993.
____
6 They grow the best coffee in Colombia.
____
7 They sold over 17 million new cars in the USA in 2018.
____
8 This factory produces 5,000 bicycles every year.
____

8B I'VE BEEN A FAN FOR 20 YEARS

1 GRAMMAR
Present perfect with *for* and *since*

a Complete the exchanges. Use the present perfect forms of the verbs in brackets and *for* or *since*.

1 A Have you always loved (you, love) horses?
B Yes, I ______ (love) horses ______ I was a little girl.

2 A ______ (you, live) in Oviedo ______ a long time?
B Yes, we ______ (live) here all our lives.

3 A How long ______ (you, be) married to Lucy?
B We ______ (be) married ______ 2005, but I ______ (know) her ______ longer.

4 A How long ______ (you, have) your stomach ache?
B I ______ (have) it ______ last night.

5 A How long ______ (you, work) as a journalist?
B I ______ (be) a journalist ______ over 20 years.

b Underline the correct words to complete the sentences.

1 We *'ve lived* / *lived* here for ten years – from 1964 to 1974.
2 I *know* / *'ve known* Sam since we went to school together.
3 My daughter *'s been* / *was* in the USA for six weeks, but she's flying home from San Francisco tomorrow.
4 She *had* / *'s had* a headache since she woke up this morning.
5 I *'ve been* / *was* in Quito since 2012, but before that I *worked* / *'ve worked* in Milan for two years.
6 John *had* / *'s had* a motorbike since he was 16 years old.

2 VOCABULARY
Sports and leisure activities

a Which verb do we use to talk about each sport and activity? Complete the chart with the words in the box.

~~gymnastics~~ squash golf surfing yoga volleyball athletics snowboarding ice skating tennis rugby football aerobics jogging ice hockey rock climbing karate skateboarding scuba diving windsurfing judo

play	go	do
		gymnastics

b 08.01 Listen and check.

c Complete the crossword puzzle.

→ Across

5 Why don't we play volleyball when we go to the beach? I've got a ball and the nets are already there.
8 The beaches in Wales are often very windy, so they're good for ______.
10 In New York, you can go ice ______ in Central Park in the winter.
11 My uncle sometimes goes rock ______ in the mountains.
12 When I'm stressed, I do ______. It helps me to relax.

↓ Down

1 I think that the most popular sport in Canada is ice ______.
2 I'm not very good at skiing, but I love ______ – it's great fun!
3 In my opinion, the best part of the Olympic Games is the ______. I love watching the 100 metres and the long jump.
4 My grandparents play ______ twice a week. They play all 18 holes, so it's a good way for them to keep fit.
6 Bondi Beach in Sydney is a great place to go ______.
7 I can't run very fast, but I like ______. Sometimes I run about four or five kilometres.
9 Have you ever been scuba ______ in the sea? I love seeing all the beautiful fish under the water.

3 PRONUNCIATION Word stress

a 08.02 Listen to the words and tick (✓) the stressed syllable in each word.

1 snowboarding
a ☑ snow b ☐ board c ☐ ing

2 athletics
a ☐ ath b ☐ let c ☐ ics

3 jogging
a ☐ jog b ☐ ging

4 gymnastics
a ☐ gym b ☐ nas c ☐ tics

5 ice hockey
a ☐ ice b ☐ hock c ☐ ey

8C EVERYDAY ENGLISH
I'm really sorry I haven't called

1 USEFUL LANGUAGE
Apologies and excuses

a Put the words in the correct order to make sentences.

1 to / to dinner / didn't / but / last week, / I / invite you / feel / I meant / well .
I meant to invite you to dinner last week, but I didn't feel well.

2 your / I couldn't / party yesterday / was / come to / ill / because / I'm sorry / I .
____

3 I / you / email / my wi-fi / because / working / couldn't / wasn't .
____

4 didn't / be late / for / to / was / the train / but / delayed / mean / I / the meeting, .
____

5 but / didn't / really sorry / were / I / buy you / I'm / the shops / closed / a present, .
____

6 working / I / call you / but / my phone / didn't / last night, / wasn't / I'm sorry .
____

7 going to / been / by today, / was / the report / but / finish / I've / I / so busy .
____

8 you / meant to / send / your address / I / find / a birthday card, / I couldn't / but .
____

b Complete the sentences with the words in the box.

fault had to mean ~~sorry~~ couldn't worry fine going to matter meant

1 I'm really *sorry* I didn't call you this morning.
2 I ________ send her any flowers for her birthday.
3 I didn't ________ to be so late.
4 It doesn't ________. It's ________.
5 I was ________ take you to a nice restaurant last night.
6 I ________ to come and visit you when you were in hospital.
7 Don't ________ about it. It wasn't your ________.
8 We were going to come yesterday, but we ________ visit our grandfather in the hospital.

2 PRONUNCIATION
Intonation for continuing or finishing

a 08.03 Listen to the sentences. Tick (✓) to show if the intonation goes up ↗ or down ↘ at the end.

	↗	↘
1 I meant to send you an email	✓	☐
2 I'm sorry I didn't come to your party	☐	☐
3 I couldn't call you last night	☐	☐
4 I had to stay late at work yesterday	☐	☐
5 Sorry, I didn't mean to make you worry	☐	☐
6 I was going to call you	☐	☐
7 I'm sorry I didn't reply to your message	☐	☐
8 I had to visit my grandmother yesterday	☐	☐

b 08.04 Does the speaker have anything more to say? Listen and check.

8D SKILLS FOR WRITING
I couldn't put the book down

1 READING

a Read the review of *Nineteen Eighty-Four* and tick (✓) the correct answer.

The reviewer thinks that …

a ☐ the book isn't very interesting.
b ☐ the book is based on a true story.
c ☐ life in Oceania is described very well.
d ☐ the ending isn't very good.

Nineteen Eighty-Four was written by George Orwell in 1948 and is set in the future, in 1984. After a nuclear war, Great Britain has become part of the totalitarian state of Oceania and everybody is controlled by the Party and its leader, Big Brother.

Although Winston Smith works for the Ministry of Truth, he secretly hates the Party and would like to oppose Big Brother. One day he meets and falls in love with Julia, a woman who also works at the Ministry of Truth and secretly hates Big Brother. However, it is very dangerous for Winston and Julia to have a relationship because love is illegal in Oceania.

Nineteen Eighty-Four is a really exciting novel. It's interesting to read and it describes the world of Oceania and Big Brother very well, so you can really imagine what life is like in a future totalitarian state after a nuclear war. Winston and Julia are wonderful characters and their illegal love affair is described very well. You can really understand how they feel.

I couldn't put the book down and I thought the ending was very clever. I would definitely recommend it. It's the best novel I've read in ages!

b Read the review of *Nineteen Eighty-Four* again. Are the sentences true (*T*) or false (*F*)?

1 ☐ Big Brother is the leader of Oceania.
2 ☐ Everybody knows that Winston hates the Party.
3 ☐ The reviewer thinks that the story is a bit boring.
4 ☐ The reviewer thinks the descriptions of people's lives in *Nineteen Eighty-Four* are very good.
5 ☐ The reviewer thinks *Nineteen Eighty-Four* is a book that other people should read.

2 WRITING SKILLS
Positive and negative comments; Linking: *although*, *however*

a Complete the sentences with *although* or *however*.

1 Although I enjoyed the novel, the story is quite complicated.
2 The descriptions of London during the war were so realistic. ________, sometimes they were a bit long and dull.
3 The story was quite exciting, ________ the book was too long for me to finish on holiday.
4 The characters were described very well. ________, there are so many of them that sometimes I forgot who they were.
5 ________ the ending was rather sad, I really enjoyed the book and would definitely recommend it.
6 It's a brilliant book, ________ the story is sometimes a little hard to follow.

3 WRITING

a Choose one of the following:

1 Write a review of a book you've read. Describe the characters, the descriptions and the story, and give your opinion of the book.
2 Read the notes below and write a review of the children's novel, *War Horse*, by Michael Morpurgo.

Notes for book review
Book: *War Horse*
Author: Michael Morpurgo
Story summary:
- about horse called Joey, sold to British Army at beginning of First World War
- sent to France, ridden by Captain Nicholls
- Captain Nicholls killed in fighting, so Joey given to a younger soldier, Warren
- J becomes friends with another horse, Topthorn: lots of adventures
- later, J and T taken by Germans
- T killed, but J works for German army until end of war

Review:
- *War Horse* written for children, but really enjoyed it
- story: very interesting
- characters: described really well
- can imagine what First World War was like
- beautiful story, but really sad: made me cry
- happy ending: at end of war J returned to Albert (his original owner before J was sold to army)
- couldn't put it down – definitely recommend …

UNIT 8
Reading and listening extension

1 READING

a Read the article from a tourist brochure. Are the sentences true (*T*) or false (*F*)?

1 ☐ The Brighton Festival is for people who like reading, listening to music and seeing films and plays.
2 ☐ It is very easy to see an event in the festival.
3 ☐ Sam Lee writes most of the songs that he sings.
4 ☐ You can see Kaarina Kaikkonen's *Time Passing By* in an art gallery.
5 ☐ *Flathampton* is a town in a theatre.

b Read the article again and complete the table to show the correct events for the sentences. Sometimes there is more than one possible answer.

	To Sleep To Dream	Sam Lee	Kaarina Kaikkonen	*Flathampton*
1 This event is outside.			✓	
2 You can listen to music from the past.				
3 There is nothing to see at this event.				
4 The audience must help the actors.				
5 This event tells a story.				

c Read the article again. Tick (✓) the correct answers.

1 The Brighton Festival …
 a ☐ is a big party that happens on Brighton beach every May.
 b ☑ happens in many places in the city, and people often have to join in.
 c ☐ happens in people's houses and is not for visitors to the city.

2 In *To Sleep To Dream*, …
 a ☐ the audience must listen very carefully.
 b ☐ the audience watches a film about music.
 c ☐ the actors can't see the audience.

3 The songs that Sam Lee sings …
 a ☐ were written while he was travelling around Britain.
 b ☐ were written by the musicians in his band.
 c ☐ were found while he was travelling around Britain.

4 *Time Passing By* …
 a ☐ is a painting of a clock in Brighton.
 b ☐ is made using things belonging to other people.
 c ☐ is a sculpture made of clocks.

5 *Flathampton* …
 a ☐ is a play where the audience helps build a town.
 b ☐ takes place in the town centre.
 c ☐ is a play about children living in a theatre.

d Write a paragraph about a festival that happens near where you live. Remember to include:

- what it is
- where it is
- what happens
- what you like and dislike about it.

THE BRIGHTON FESTIVAL

If you like music, going to art galleries, the cinema or the theatre, or learning about books, then you really should visit the Brighton Festival. It has been going since 1965 and is now one of the largest arts festivals in England.

Come to Brighton in May and it's impossible not to see something as events, such as plays, concerts, films, dance performances and exhibitions take place across the city in cinemas, theatres, galleries, the street, on the beach and even in people's own houses.

There have been some amazing events. Here are some of the highlights from the last two years:

Sam Lee is a singer who has spent many years travelling around Britain to find and listen to very old British songs. Many of the songs were written hundreds of years ago and he performs them with an interesting band of musicians.

Kaarina Kaikkonen is a Finnish artist who often uses other people's clothes to make large sculptures. In *Time Passing By*, the 23-metre-high Clock Tower in the city centre was covered in clothes. It was very popular with visitors and artists.

In *To Sleep To Dream*, which was written by Daniel Clark, everyone in the audience wears a blindfold (something that covers the eyes so you can't see) to help them concentrate on the story, which is told with special 3D sound effects and music. In this film for the ears, your ears become your eyes.

Flathampton is a play with a difference. The whole theatre is turned into a town and the audience are taken through the town by the actors. As the story is told, the audience have to help make the buildings in the town that the actors perform in. It's been extremely popular with children and adults alike.

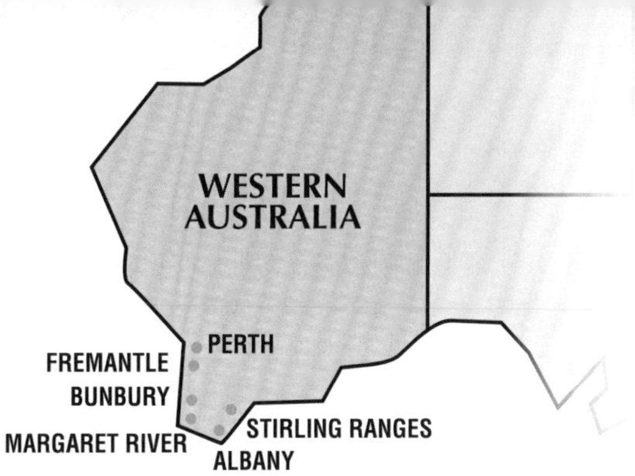

2 LISTENING

a 08.05 Listen to the radio programme and look at the map of western Australia. Complete the table to show where the activities are. Sometimes there is more than one possible answer.

	Stirling Ranges	Perth	Near Fremantle	Bunbury	Margaret River
1 This is for people who enjoy watching foreign films.		✓			
2 This is not for beginners.					
3 This is for people who don't mind getting wet.					
4 A lot of people will do this on Sunday morning.					
5 A group of young people will perform on a beach.					
6 This is for people who like sport.					

b 08.05 Listen again. Underline the correct words to complete the sentences.

1 If you want to know where to go rock climbing at the Stirling Ranges, you can *look on the website* / *visit the information centre* / *visit your local bookshop or library*.
2 *The sea* / *The day* / *The river* affects where Margaret River Surfers meet.
3 The photographs in the art gallery in Perth were taken by *photographers* / *film directors* / *actors*.
4 On the beach at Wilson Park, you can *listen to* / *write* / *read* poems by young poets.
5 *Jenny* / *Matt* / *Virginia* is going to be doing something active with a large group this weekend.

c Write about your hobbies. Remember to include:

- what you like doing
- how long you've been doing this
- where you do this
- who you do it with.

Review and extension

1 GRAMMAR

Correct the sentences.

1 The Harry Potter books weren't written of Charles Dickens.
The Harry Potter books weren't written by Charles Dickens.
2 I knew Veronica since I was a child.
3 We've lived in Edirne since more than ten years.
4 The Sydney Opera House is designed by Jørn Utzon.
5 I have taught at that university from 2016 to 2019.
6 I have played golf from I was 12 years old.

2 VOCABULARY

Correct the sentences.

1 This morning we played volley at the beach.
This morning we played volleyball at the beach.
2 Skateboard is a great way for children to get fit.
3 Have you got a fotograph of your girlfriend?
4 Let's play golfing this afternoon.
5 These days, ice skate is popular in New York City during the winter.
6 When I was at school, I had to do gymnastic every Wednesday.
7 The *Mona Lisa* is one of the most famous paints in the world.
8 Let's do surfing this afternoon.

3 WORDPOWER *by*

Complete the sentences with the words in the box.

bus next Monday hand mistake heart ~~the library~~ far the way

1 She's waiting for you by *the library*.
2 By ____________, are you doing anything on Friday?
3 Sorry, I clicked SEND by ____________ before I finished writing the email.
4 I usually come to work by ____________.
5 Actors have to learn their lines by ____________.
6 These shoes were made by ____________. That's why they're more expensive.
7 Usain Bolt is by ____________ the best 100-metres runner of the past 15 years.
8 Please send me your report by ____________.

REVIEW YOUR PROGRESS

Look again at Review Your Progress on p. 86 of the Student's Book. How well can you do these things now?
3 = very well 2 = well 1 = not so well

I CAN ...	
talk about art, music and literature	☐
talk about sports and leisure activities	☐
apologise and make and accept excuses	☐
write a book review.	☐

9A IF I DON'T PASS THIS EXAM, I WON'T BE VERY HAPPY

1 VOCABULARY Degree subjects; Education collocations

a Complete the crossword puzzle.

→ Across

2 If you want to become a doctor, you'll have to study m<u>edicine</u> at university.

3 He went to university to study d__________ and then got a job as an actor.

4 If you study l__________ at university, you will learn everything about our legal system.

5 She studied e__________ at university, and now she's helping design a new bridge across the Guadalquivir River in Spain.

7 He did a degree in a__________, and now he does beautiful drawings for children's books.

↓ Down

1 He was really interested in other people and how they think, so he decided to study p__________.

2 If you want to become a manager in a large company, you should do a degree in business m__________.

6 She's doing a degree in e__________ because she wants to become a teacher.

b Complete the sentences with the words in the box.

degree	get	notes	pass	revise	place
fail	essays	~~marks~~	handed		

1 He got really low <u>marks</u> in his exams, so he's going to repeat the year.

2 She did a __________ in French and Spanish, and now she works as a tour guide.

3 I've got to write three __________ before the end of term, and each one is 4,000 words long.

4 If she doesn't work hard this term, I think she might __________ her exams.

5 I've got to __________ for an important exam, so I won't go out today or tomorrow.

6 Because he __________ in his essay two days late, he only got 45%.

7 I didn't take a pen and paper with me to the meeting, but I took some __________ on my laptop.

8 He did extremely well in his exams and got a __________ at Harvard University.

9 Your daughter has always worked hard, so she'll definitely __________ into university.

10 You should study several hours every day if you want to __________ your exams.

2 GRAMMAR First conditional

a Put the words in the correct order to make sentences.

1 it / tomorrow, / we're / If / to / go skiing / going / snows .
<u>If it snows tomorrow, we're going to go skiing.</u>

2 if / I'll / Canada / to / can / on holiday / I / a / cheap flight / find / go .
____

3 might / they / every day, / revise / they / their exams / If / pass .
____

4 at / If / her exams, / might / a place / she / in / Cambridge University / she / does well / get .
____

5 medicine / have to / excellent marks / get / if / She'll / to study / wants / at university / she .
____

6 call / tonight / tomorrow morning / him / if / doesn't / to / my email / I'll / reply / he .
____

7 on time / give / don't / you / bad mark / if / might / hand in / a / you / essay / Your teacher / your .
____

8 fail / university / your exams, / you / you / If / get into / won't .
____

3 PRONUNCIATION Word groups

a 09.01 Listen to the sentences and mark // where there is a pause.

1 I enjoy studying maths at university, // but I hate taking exams.

2 If you take notes in the lesson, it will be easier to revise for the exam.

3 I'm going to work harder next year so that I get better grades.

4 If she fails her exam, she'll have to take it again in January.

5 Although he got excellent grades, he didn't get a place at Oxford University.

9B I MANAGED TO STOP FEELING SHY

1 GRAMMAR Verb patterns

a Underline the correct words to complete the sentences.

1 I usually finish *to play* / *playing* / *play* tennis at about nine o'clock.
2 We decided *not taking* / *not to take* / *to not take* the next train to Rome.
3 He keeps *to try* / *try* / *trying* to learn Portuguese, but he always gives up.
4 We wanted *see* / *to see* / *seeing* the film, but there were no tickets left.
5 She promised *to not fail* / *not failing* / *not to fail* any exams this year.
6 I don't mind *not to take* / *to not take* / *not taking* a holiday this year if we can take one next year.
7 They learned *to speak* / *speaking* / *speak* English by talking to their grandfather.
8 I hope *go* / *to go* / *going* on holiday to Thailand next summer.
9 I really enjoy *to spend* / *spend* / *spending* time with my family.
10 I worry about *to not do* / *not do* / *not doing* well in the exams, but I always pass.

b Complete the sentences with the correct forms of the verbs in the box.

meet get go take snow ~~buy~~ read play

1 He promised __to buy__ her a new phone if she got good marks in her exams.
2 We decided ________ the bus because the train was a lot more expensive.
3 I really enjoy ________ to the theatre when I'm in London.
4 She expected ________ a good result, but she didn't.
5 My sisters and I used to love ________ games on the beach when we were little.
6 She's arranged ________ him at the check-in desk at the airport.
7 He finished ________ his book and then went to bed.
8 It started ________ heavily last night and now they've closed the airport.

2 VOCABULARY Verbs followed by *to* + infinitive / verb + *-ing*

a Complete the sentences with the words in the box.

forgot avoid regretted seemed agreed managed ~~arranged~~ recommended disliked missed refused imagined

1 They __arranged__ to meet their friends outside the cinema at 7:30.
2 When we asked the tour guide, he ________ taking a taxi to the beach.
3 Because she was shy, she ________ meeting new people at parties.
4 She ________ to take her purse to the restaurant, so her boyfriend had to pay the bill.
5 Fortunately, the taxi driver ________ to drive us to the airport when we offered him 50 euros.
6 He ________ buying a house by the sea. He thought it would be lovely to walk on the beach every day.
7 After she moved from the USA to Mexico, she really ________ seeing her family in the summer.
8 I went to work early this morning because I wanted to ________ driving in the city centre during rush hour.
9 Most of the hotels were full, but in the end we ________ to find a nice hotel near the beach.
10 When she got low marks in her exams, she ________ not working harder.
11 The hotel receptionist ________ to understand what I was saying because she brought some sandwiches to our room five minutes later.
12 He ________ to give the waiter a tip because the service was so slow.

b Underline the correct words to complete the sentences.

1 She has *avoided* / *agreed* / *missed* to meet Luke for coffee after work.
2 He usually *avoids* / *missed* / *recommends* speaking to his neighbours because he's rather shy.
3 Let's *refuse* / *forget* / *arrange* to have dinner together one evening this week.
4 I'm sorry, but I *managed* / *forgot* / *refused* to get any bread when I was at the supermarket.
5 She *regrets* / *avoids* / *recommends* going to the Alhambra Palace in Granada. She says it's beautiful.
6 Now that you live in a flat, do you *miss* / *regret* / *imagine* having a garden?
7 I don't want to go to the party, so if they ask me to go with them, I will politely *forget* / *manage* / *refuse*.
8 She *imagined* / *disliked* / *recommended* swimming in the sea because the water was always so cold.
9 Our baby *seems* / *manages* / *refuses* to prefer classical music to pop music.
10 Did you *refuse* / *manage* / *seem* to get some tickets to the concert? They almost sold out on the first day.

9C EVERYDAY ENGLISH
Who's calling, please?

1 USEFUL LANGUAGE Phoning people you know; Phoning people you don't know

a Put the conversation in the correct order.

A Is it possible to speak to Diane Smith, please?
B Certainly. I'll just put you through.

- [ ] **C** Has she got your number?
- [ ] **C** OK. Shall I ask her to call you back?
- [ ] **C** No, I'm afraid she isn't available. She's in a meeting. Can I take a message?
- [ ] **A** Oh, hello. Is Diane there, please?
- [ ] **C** Yes, of course. Who's calling, please?
- [ ] **A** Yes, OK. Can you tell her that I called?
- [ ] **A** Yes, please. I'm here all morning.
- [1] **C** Hello, Diane Smith's phone.
- [ ] **A** This is Paul Roberts speaking.
- [ ] **A** Yes, she has.

C Fine. I'll ask her to call you back.
A Thanks. Bye.

b 09.02 Listen and check.

c Complete the conversation with the words in the box.

got to go I've got ~~is that~~ it's just saying soon catch that call you back call good time it is

PAM Oh, hello, [1] _is that_ Tom?
TOM Yes, [2] ________.
PAM Hi, [3] ________ Pam here.
TOM Oh, hi, Pam.
PAM Is now a [4] ________ to talk?
TOM Well, I'm a bit busy.
PAM Sorry, Tom, I didn't [5] ________.
TOM Yes, I was [6] ________ that I'm busy. Sorry, but [7] ________ a meeting in five minutes. Can I [8] ________?
PAM Sure. Is everything OK?
TOM Yes, fine, but I've [9] ________.
PAM OK. [10] ________ me when you're free.
TOM Speak to you [11] ________. Bye.
PAM Bye.

d 09.03 Listen and check.

2 PRONUNCIATION Main stress: contrastive

a 09.04 We can use contrastive stress to correct something someone else has said. Listen to the pairs of sentences. In each pair, check (✓) the sentence where you hear a strong stress.

1 a [ ] The film starts at 8:50.
  b [✓] The film starts at 8:15.
2 a [ ] We're catching the nine o'clock bus.
  b [ ] We're catching the ten o'clock bus.
3 a [ ] My new boyfriend's name is James.
  b [ ] My new boyfriend's name is John.
4 a [ ] The programme is on BBC 1.
  b [ ] The programme is on BBC 2.
5 a [ ] We're going on holiday on Tuesday.
  b [ ] We're going on holiday on Thursday.
6 a [ ] I was born in 1990.
  b [ ] I was born in 1991.

9D SKILLS FOR WRITING

Online learning is new to me

1 READING

a Read the profile of a French student and tick (✓) the correct answer.

a ☐ Claude's studying French.
b ☐ Claude's going to study in the USA next year.
c ☐ The online course is about American cinema.
d ☐ Claude works in a café every day.

b Read Claude's profile again. Are the sentences true (*T*) or false (*F*)?

1 ☐ Claude likes the subjects he's doing at university.
2 ☐ He already speaks and writes English very well.
3 ☐ He hopes he will be better at writing in English after the online course.
4 ☐ He wants to make friends with American students.
5 ☐ He doesn't often go to watch films with his friends in Paris.

TELL US ABOUT YOU ...

Hi, everyone. My name's Claude and I'm French. I'm doing an English and German degree at the Sorbonne University here in Paris. I'm really enjoying it. At the moment, I'm studying 20th-century American novelists, such as Ernest Hemingway. It's really interesting, but the best thing about my degree is that next year I'll spend six months in the UK and six months in Germany – I can't wait! I also get the chance to take an online course in film studies. I can already speak English very well because my father's American. However, my written English isn't very good.

HOW DO YOU FEEL ABOUT THIS ONLINE COURSE?

I've always loved the cinema, so I'm really looking forward to taking this American film studies course. I hope it will help me understand American films better and improve my written English at the same time. I'm also very excited about making friends with students from different countries.

WHAT DO YOU DO WHEN YOU'RE NOT STUDYING?

I have a part-time job in a café near the Arc de Triomphe, in the heart of Paris. I work there three evenings a week and sometimes on Sundays, too. In my free time, I like going out with my friends. We usually go to the cinema, or sometimes we have dinner in one of the cheap restaurants in the Latin Quarter.

2 WRITING SKILLS Avoiding repetition

a Change the words in **bold** in the sentences to pronouns.

1 I'm doing a degree in medicine. I'm really enjoying **my degree** ___it___.
2 The other students on my course all come from different countries. **The other students** ______ all speak English very well.
3 My cousin Paola is also studying at the same university as me. **Paola's** ______ doing a degree in business administration.
4 When I'm not studying, I spend time with my girlfriend, Anna. I see **Anna** ______ three or four times a week.
5 We haven't decided which hotel to stay at when we go to Rome. I think we should try and find **a hotel** ______ near the Colosseum.
6 My dad's an IT consultant. **My dad** ______ usually works from home, but sometimes **my dad** ______ has to go to Birmingham for meetings.
7 My brother and I are both studying law. My parents have always wanted **my brother and I** ______ to become lawyers, just like my father.
8 I have a part-time job working in a supermarket. **This part-time job** ______ isn't very interesting, but I do **this part-time job** ______ because I need the money.

3 WRITING

a Read the notes and write a student profile for Hitomi, who is also taking the online American film studies course.

Student profile – notes

Tell us about you ...
- Hitomi: from Osaka, Japan
- Master's degree in economics – Tokyo University
- next year: job in London or New York?
- studied English at school: writing OK, but speaking???

How do you feel about this online course?
- want to learn about Am. films: always loved Am. films
- improve English?
- talk about films with other students?
- my English: improve quickly?

What do you do when you're not studying?

sport – tennis x1 or x2 a week
– golf at weekends
– gym at the university: like keeping fit
– yoga when stressed: helps me relax

UNIT 9
Reading and listening extension

1 READING

a Read the text. Complete the sentences with the subjects in the box.

~~business~~ law medicine psychology

1 More foreign students study business than any other subject.
2 Sanoh is doing a degree in ______.
3 Onur is studying ______.
4 Roberto is studying ______.

b Read the text again. Tick (✓) the correct answers.

1 The country with the most foreign students studying at its universities is …
a ☐ China.
b ☐ the UK
c ☑ the USA
2 According to the British Council, the number of foreign students studying in the UK in ten years' time will be …
a ☐ more than 126,000.
b ☐ 430,000.
c ☐ more than half a million.
3 Sanoh wanted to come to the UK …
a ☐ a long time ago.
b ☐ to study English.
c ☐ to find a job.
4 Onur decided to go to the UK because …
a ☐ he went to school there.
b ☐ he knows the country well.
c ☐ he wanted to study law.
5 How does Roberto feel about being in Bath?
a ☐ He would like to be somewhere else.
b ☐ He would like to stay there longer.
c ☐ He prefers the food in Ecuador.

c Read the text again and complete the sentences.

1 If Onur doesn't pass his exams, he will have to repeat his classes.
2 Sanoh imagined going to ______ for a long time.
3 Roberto went to England because he ______ English.
4 Sanoh has recommended ______ in Edinburgh to friends of hers.
5 Roberto will try to find ______ in Bath if he does well in his final exams.

d Write a paragraph about your experiences studying. Remember to include:

- what you've studied
- where you've studied
- which exams you've taken
- what you like and dislike about studying.

Studying in the UK

Over 430,000 foreign students from nearly 200 countries study at universities in the UK, with the largest number, over 78,000, coming from China. Only the USA takes more foreign students.

The most popular courses for foreign students are business management and engineering. Over 130,000 of those students do a degree in business and more than 50,000 study engineering in the UK.

A recent report by the British Council (a UK government organisation interested in British education and culture) suggests that over the next ten years an additional 126,000 international students will come to the UK to study. What makes the UK such an attractive place to study?

Sanoh, 19, Thailand
I decided to study in the UK because I love reading British novels, and I've always dreamed about coming here. I applied to five universities here and got a place at Edinburgh to study medicine. I'm really happy with the course and I've met a lot of students from all over the world. Edinburgh is a fun city and I've already told my friends who would like to study abroad next year how great it is.

Onur, 20, Turkey
I studied at an international school in Istanbul and I've been to the UK many times. I have family in Cardiff, so it seemed to be a good choice for me. I'm studying law. I have to write a lot of essays. At the end of the year I need to hand in three long essays and also pass my exams. I hope I manage to do everything. Failing the exams means repeating the year. I don't want to do that!

Roberto, 21, Ecuador
I wanted to study abroad and because English is the only foreign language I speak, I decided to come here. I'm happy I came to Bath. The weather, the culture and the food are very different from my home town of Quito, but the city is beautiful and the people are really friendly. I'm studying for my final exams in psychology at the moment. If I pass, I'll probably stay here and look for a job.

2 LISTENING

a 09.05 Listen to the conversation. Are the sentences true (*T*) or false (*F*)?

1 ☐ Gavino has written six essays this term.
2 ☐ Gavino is in his first year at university.
3 ☐ Gavino was late for class for two weeks.
4 ☐ Gavino failed his exams.
5 ☐ Gavino studies for the exam every Wednesday.
6 ☐ There are 25 students studying psychology in Gavino's year.

b 09.05 Listen to the conversation again. Match 1–6 with a–f to make sentences.

1 [b] The professor isn't going to mark Gavino's essay if
2 ☐ If Gavino doesn't come to class,
3 ☐ Gavino didn't go to some classes because
4 ☐ Gavino might not pass the exam if
5 ☐ Gavino might not be in the psychology course next year if
6 ☐ The professor is not happy with Gavino because

a he doesn't go to every class.
b he doesn't hand it in on time.
c he fails the exam.
d he hasn't read any of the books.
e he was ill.
f he won't learn anything.

c Write about how you revise for an exam. Remember to include:

- how long you spend revising
- what you do to help remember information
- how good you are at doing exams.

Review and extension

1 GRAMMAR

Correct the sentences.

1 If I'll work hard, I'll pass the exam.
If I work hard, I'll pass the exam.
2 I want that you buy me some bread and milk from the shop.
3 We won't play golf this afternoon if it will rain.
4 She enjoys to read books about dinosaurs.
5 Will you go to university next year if you'll get good marks?
6 I've just finished to have dinner with my family.

2 VOCABULARY

Correct the sentences.

1 When Robert left England to go and live in Australia, he regretted seeing his friends from home.
When Robert left England to go and live in Australia, he missed seeing his friends from home.
2 He did well really at school and got into a good university.
3 She got a very bad note on her last history essay.
4 Although they worked hard, they both fell their maths exams.
5 She always took taxis because she misliked waiting for buses.
6 He made a degree in medicine and now he's a doctor.

3 WORDPOWER
Multi-word verbs with *put*

Complete the sentences with the prepositions in the box.

on down away off ~~back~~

1 Please put the milk _back_ in the fridge when you're finished with it.
2 They'll put ________ their notes after they finish studying.
3 OK, everybody. The exam is finished now, so please put your pens ________ and stop writing. Thank you.
4 It's raining quite hard now. Why don't we put ________ our game of tennis until tomorrow?
5 I usually put ________ a suit when I go for a job interview.

REVIEW YOUR PROGRESS

Look again at Review Your Progress on p. 96 of the Student's Book. How well can you do these things now?
3 = very well 2 = well 1 = not so well

I CAN ...	
talk about future possibilities	☐
describe actions and feelings	☐
make telephone calls	☐
write a personal profile.	☐

10A WOULD YOU DO THE RIGHT THING?

1 GRAMMAR Second conditional

a Put the words in the correct order to make sentences.

1 I / to the police station / If / take it / found some money / in the street, / I'd .
<u>If I found some money in the street, I'd take it to the police station.</u>

2 complain / the waiter / you / with your bill / Would / if / made a mistake ?
____

3 would / at school / there were / do / What / if / no teachers / you ?
____

4 I / I could / on petrol / cycled to work, / a lot of money / If / save .
____

5 did yoga / I / feel / every day / less stressed / I / would / if .
____

6 take a taxi / If / the last bus, / I'd /missed / have to / I .
____

7 if / I / could stop / became rich / working / I .
____

8 you / would / the film / download it / you / on the Internet, / found / If ?
____

b <u>Underline</u> the correct words to make second conditional sentences.

1 If I *would be* / <u>*were*</u> / *am* you, I *will buy* / *bought* / <u>*would buy*</u> her some flowers.
2 *Could you work* / *Will you work* / *Did you work* seven days a week if you *need* / *needed* / *would need* the money?
3 If the shop assistant *would be* / *was* / *will be* rude to me, *I'm complaining* / *I complained* / *I'd complain* to the manager.
4 *I could take* / *I'll take* / *I took* you to the bus station if my car *isn't* / *wasn't* / *wouldn't be* at the garage.
5 If you *will walk* / *would walk* / *walked* five kilometres every day, *you feel* / *you felt* / *you'd feel* much healthier.
6 If my new watch *stopped* / *will stop* / *would stop* working after two weeks, I *'ll take* / *'d take* / *take* it back to the shop.
7 I *didn't walk* / *wouldn't walk* / *won't walk* home by myself if I *am* / *would be* / *were* you.
8 What *did you do* / *do you do* / *would you do* if you *lost* / *would lose* / *will lose* your car keys?

2 VOCABULARY Multi-word verbs

a Match 1–8 with a–h to make sentences.

1 [h] Could you pass
2 [ ] Why don't you come
3 [ ] At some hotels, you have to hand
4 [ ] My neighbour joined
5 [ ] Because they were very tired, they didn't feel
6 [ ] I asked him to speak in English, but he carried
7 [ ] His mother looked
8 [ ] He was offered a great job, but he turned it

a down because he didn't want to leave Italy.
b after him when he was ill last week.
c in our game of volleyball.
d in your passport when you first arrive.
e on speaking in German, so I couldn't understand him.
f like going to the cinema, so they watched a film on TV.
g round to my house for dinner on Saturday?
h on my complaint to the manager, please?

b <u>Underline</u> the correct words to complete the sentences.

1 It's very rude to carry *in* / <u>*on*</u> / *after* talking when the film starts.
2 When Jack lost his job, they decided to put *up* / *on* / *off* their wedding until he could find another one.
3 My neighbour came *round* / *after* / *to* for a cup of coffee this morning.
4 If you don't feel *down* / *like* / *off* eating much, just have some fruit.
5 My sister's sad because she and her boyfriend broke *down* / *off* / *up* yesterday.
6 I found someone's phone under my desk, so I handed it *in* / *on* / *up* to my teacher.
7 Who's going to look *up* / *for* / *after* your grandfather while your grandmother's away?
8 Can you pass *up* / *on* / *in* my message to Mr Henderson when he gets back on Monday, please?

3 PRONUNCIATION Sentence stress: vowel sounds

a 10.01 Listen to the sentences and tick (✓) if the words in **bold** are stressed or unstressed.

	Stressed	Unstressed
1 If I had lots of money, I **would** buy an expensive sports car.	☐	☑
2 **Would** you marry him if he didn't live so far away?	☐	☐
3 If I were you, I **wouldn't** go swimming in the sea today.	☐	☐
4 If he asked her to go to Argentina with him, she probably **would**.	☐	☐
5 I **would** come and stay with you in New York if the flights weren't so expensive.	☐	☐
6 She **wouldn't** have to drive to work every day if she lived closer to her office.	☐	☐

10B I'M TOO EMBARRASSED TO COMPLAIN

1 GRAMMAR
Quantifiers; *too / not enough*

a Underline the correct words to complete the conversation.

A We'll need [1]*much* / *a lot of* / *any* flour, sugar and, of course, carrots to make this cake. We'll also need [2]*a little* / *many* / *a few* orange juice.
B Well, there's [3]*any* / *no* / *many* flour in the cupboard, so I'll have to go and buy some.
A Good idea. So, what else do we need? Er, butter … how [4]*many* / *few* / *much* butter have we got in the fridge?
B Er, we haven't got [5]*many* / *much* / *some* butter. Just one packet – 250 grams.
A OK, that's fine. And what about eggs – how [6]*many* / *much* / *any* eggs are there?
B There aren't [7]*much* / *many* / *any* eggs – only four.
A OK. And have we got [8]*much* / *a little* / *any* carrots?
B Yes, I think we have [9]*a few* / *much* / *few* carrots, maybe three or four. Let me just check … oh, actually, there aren't [10]*any* / *many* / *much* carrots. I think I ate the last one yesterday. Sorry!
A Never mind. OK, so can you also get me [11]*any* / *some* / *a little* carrots from the supermarket, please?
B OK, you'd better write me a shopping list …

b Underline the correct words to complete the sentences.

1 I couldn't have a shower this morning because the water wasn't *enough warm* / *warm enough*.
2 There's *too much* / *too many* sugar in my coffee now – it's disgusting!
3 I'm sorry, I haven't got *enough milk* / *milk enough* to make coffee for everyone.
4 You're driving *too much* / *too* slowly – we won't get to the airport on time!
5 You aren't speaking *enough clearly* / *clearly enough*. I can't understand you.
6 There are *too many* / *too much* cars in the city these days. The traffic's always terrible!
7 You're walking *too much quickly* / *too quickly* for me. I can't walk as fast as you.
8 My flat isn't *enough big* / *big enough* to have a birthday party for all my friends.

2 VOCABULARY Noun formation

a Complete the crossword puzzle.

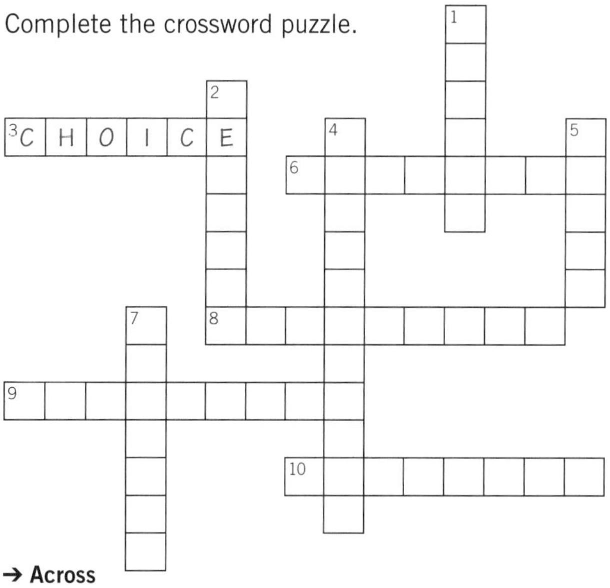

→ Across
3 There isn't much c*hoice* in the little supermarket near my house. For example, they only have two types of bread.
6 The directors made the d__________ to sell the company.
8 I buy books online. They're usually d__________ to my house within three or four days.
9 Excuse me. I'd like to make a formal c__________ about the quality of the food in this hotel.
10 I think people should always c__________ in a restaurant if the service is bad.

↓ Down
1 So you've ordered a new phone. What colour did you c__________ – black or white?
2 I've d__________ to redecorate my kitchen, so I've just been to the shop to buy some paint.
4 Our hotel was really horrible. It didn't match the d__________ they gave on their website.
5 Did you e__________ the new Disney film?
7 Why has the flight to Rio de Janeiro been delayed by five hours? Can you e__________ that to me?

3 PRONUNCIATION Word stress

a Tick (✓) the correct stress marking for each word.

1 decision
  a ✓ decision
  b ☐ decision
2 enjoyment
  a ☐ enjoyment
  b ☐ enjoyment
3 complaint
  a ☐ complaint
  b ☐ complaint
4 description
  a ☐ description
  b ☐ description
5 explanation
  a ☐ explanation
  b ☐ explanation
6 delivery
  a ☐ delivery
  b ☐ delivery
7 describe
  a ☐ describe
  b ☐ describe
8 complain
  a ☐ complain
  b ☐ complain

b ▶ 10.02 Listen and check.

10C EVERYDAY ENGLISH
Can I exchange it for something else?

1 USEFUL LANGUAGE Returning goods and making complaints

a Put the conversation in the correct order.

CUSTOMER Good morning. Could you help me, please?
SHOP ASSISTANT Yes, of course. How can I help?

☐ **CUSTOMER** Could I speak to the manager, please?
1 **CUSTOMER** I'd like to return this speaker, please.
☐ **SHOP ASSISTANT** Do you have a receipt?
☐ **SHOP ASSISTANT** Would you like to exchange it for something else?
☐ **SHOP ASSISTANT** Well, I'm terribly sorry, but we don't give refunds without a receipt.
☐ **CUSTOMER** No, I'm sorry, I don't. It was a present from my boyfriend, but the sound quality is very bad.
☐ **SHOP ASSISTANT** Yes, of course. I'll go and get him.
☐ **CUSTOMER** No, I'd just like a refund, please.

MANAGER What seems to be the problem?
CUSTOMER I'd like to make a complaint.

b 10.03 Listen and check.

c Put the words in the correct order to make sentences.

1 but / excuse me, / ordered / isn't / what / this / I .
Excuse me, but this isn't what I ordered.
2 ask / right away / I'll / that for / you / someone / to look at .
______
3 been here / still haven't / ordered / we've / but / for over an hour, / we .
______
4 they're / because / small / don't / these shoes / me / fit / a bit .
______
5 mind, / I've / my / I've decided / keep it / changed / and / to .
______
6 to / I'd / for / exchange it / something else / like .
______
7 please / I'd / to / this watch, / return / like .
______
8 full refund / a / give / I'll / you .
______
9 hasn't been / helpful / sales assistant / your / very .
______

d 10.04 Listen and check.

2 PRONUNCIATION Sentence stress

a 10.05 Listen and decide where the main stress is in each question. Tick (✓) the stressed word.

1 Can you check my bill, please?
a ☐ Can b ☑ check
2 Would you like me to give you a refund?
a ☐ like b ☐ give
3 Did you bring your receipt with you?
a ☐ bring b ☐ receipt
4 Where did you buy it?
a ☐ Where b ☐ buy
5 Could you wait a moment, please?
a ☐ Could b ☐ wait
6 Can you take our order now, please?
a ☐ take b ☐ order
7 Can I exchange these jeans for another pair?
a ☐ Can b ☐ exchange
8 Could you call the manager, please?
a ☐ call b ☐ manager

10D SKILLS FOR WRITING
We're really sorry we missed it

1 READING

a Read the three emails and tick (✓) the correct answers.

	Email A	Email B	Email C
1 Which email is about changing the date of a meeting?	☐	☐	☐
2 Which email is about some problems with a family holiday?	☐	☐	☐
3 Which email is from the parents of a child who was ill?	☐	☐	☐

Email A

Dear Mr Patterson,

Thank you for your email of 5 September about the problems you had on your holiday with Turkish Sun Tours. I am writing to apologise for putting you in a different hotel from your friends. Unfortunately, our agents in Turkey made a mistake with your booking and did not reserve enough rooms at Hotel Paradise. This is why they had to put you and your family in another hotel in the same resort.

I hope you will book a holiday with us again in the future and we would like to offer you a 25% discount on your next holiday with us. This is our way of apologising for the problems you had.

Yours sincerely,

Sam Polat

Customer Services Manager, Turkish Sun Tours

Email B

Hi Jim,

Just a quick message to say I'm sorry that we couldn't come to your house for dinner last Saturday. Unfortunately, our youngest son, Jack, had a really high temperature, so we couldn't leave him with our babysitter.

Some friends of ours are coming round for lunch next Sunday, so if you're free maybe you and Sarah could join us? Let me know if you can come. Hope to see you on Sunday.

Love,

Melanie

Email C

Dear Malcolm,

I'm writing to let you know that I need to rearrange my trip to New York, planned for next week. David Smith, our new managing director, has just asked me to go with him to Beijing on Sunday to attend a meeting with our Chinese distributor. I'm very sorry to cancel my trip at the last minute, but the meeting in China is really important.

Could we hold a meeting in New York the week of 15 May instead? Let me know if you're free to meet that week.

Best,

Amanda

b Read the three emails again. Are the sentences true (*T*) or false (*F*)?

1 ☐ Mr Patterson didn't stay in the same hotel as his friends.
2 ☐ The agents in Turkey couldn't find a hotel for Mr Patterson's family.
3 ☐ Turkish Sun Tours is going to give Mr Patterson a free holiday.
4 ☐ Melanie would like to invite Jim and Sarah to lunch next Sunday.
5 ☐ Amanda wants to meet Malcolm in Beijing next week.

2 WRITING SKILLS
Formal and informal language

a Read the sentences from an email from the manager of a restaurant to an unhappy customer. Rewrite the sentences and change the words in **bold** to make the email more formal.

1 **Hi** Mrs Miller,
Dear Mrs Miller,
2 **Thanks** very much for your email of 15 June.
3 **I'm** writing to **say sorry** for the poor service you received in our restaurant last Saturday.
4 **We've** just opened the restaurant, and **we've** had a few problems finding experienced waiters.
5 However, **we're** working hard to improve our levels of service and **I'm** confident that we **won't** have any more problems like this in the future.
6 We hope **you'll** come back to our restaurant again and **we'd** like to offer you a 50% discount on your next meal with us.
7 This is our way of **saying sorry** for the problems **you've** had.
8 **Best wishes,**

3 WRITING

a Read the email from David Hurst to a hotel in Nerja, Spain. Write an email of apology from the manager of the hotel. Use the notes to help you.

RE: Problems at Hotel Dante

Dear Sir/Madam,

I am writing to complain about the poor service I received when I stayed at your hotel in Nerja last week.

Firstly, when I booked the room online, I asked for a room with a sea view. However, I was given a room with a view of the car park. Secondly, the receptionist was very rude to my wife when she had a problem with the shower. In fact, there wasn't enough hot water for us to have a shower for the first two days of our stay. Finally, the service in the restaurant was too slow. Every morning we had to wait at least half an hour for our breakfast.

I look forward to hearing from you.

Yours faithfully,

David Hurst

Notes for reply to Mr Hurst

- *apologise for poor service*
- *wrong room: problems with website?*
- *shower: problems with water heating system*
- *slow service in restaurant: three waiters ill that week*
- *offer a 50% discount on next visit?*

UNIT 10
Reading and listening extension

1 READING

a Read the magazine article. Match the people 1–3 with the phrases a–c.

1 Banu	a too difficult
2 Eduardo	b concentrate better
3 Carla	c more relaxed

b Read the article again and tick (✓) the correct endings to the sentences.

1 In the magazine article, three people were asked …
 a [ ] what they thought about smartphones and technology.
 b [✓] not to use their smartphone for a week.
 c [ ] to imagine a world without technology.

2 Banu thought that she would …
 a [ ] not be involved with other people if she didn't have her phone.
 b [ ] break up with her boyfriend if she didn't have her phone.
 c [ ] enjoy not having to use her phone.

3 Banu realised that …
 a [ ] she didn't have enough time to spend with her friends.
 b [ ] she thought less about what other people were doing when she didn't have her phone.
 c [ ] she wasn't talking to her friends enough.

4 If Eduardo didn't have his phone, …
 a [ ] he thought there would be serious problems with his business.
 b [ ] he thought he would have to work more in the evenings.
 c [ ] he wouldn't be able to make decisions.

5 Carla didn't want to stop using her phone because …
 a [ ] she liked using it to read about fashion.
 b [ ] she needed it for her job.
 c [ ] she was worried that people wouldn't call her.

c Read the article again and tick (✓) the correct people. Sometimes there is more than one possible answer.

1 Who had a better private life without a smartphone?
 a [✓] Banu b [✓] Eduardo c [ ] Carla
2 Who thought they wouldn't be able to take care of something properly without their phone?
 a [ ] Banu b [ ] Eduardo c [ ] Carla
3 Who realised that they didn't have to do things immediately?
 a [ ] Banu b [ ] Eduardo c [ ] Carla
4 Who was right to be worried about not having a phone?
 a [ ] Banu b [ ] Eduardo c [ ] Carla
5 Who realised that their social life would continue without a phone?
 a [ ] Banu b [ ] Eduardo c [ ] Carla
6 Who learned something positive from the experiment?
 a [ ] Banu b [ ] Eduardo c [ ] Carla
7 Who didn't complete the experiment?
 a [ ] Banu b [ ] Eduardo c [ ] Carla
8 Who found that not communicating was a problem for their work?
 a [ ] Banu b [ ] Eduardo c [ ] Carla

d Write about what you would do if you couldn't use your phone for a week.

- How would you communicate with friends?
- How would you feel?
- What would the advantages and disadvantages be?

Please Turn Off Your Phones!

In the world today, over 3 billion (3,000,000,000) people own a smartphone, and over 80% of them say that they never turn it off. We use smartphones for everything, from making phone calls to being our personal fitness trainers. With over 5,000,000 apps available, it seems that there isn't much they can't do.

But imagine if you had to live without your smartphone for a week. What would you do?

We asked three users to try.

BANU, 19, STUDENT, ISTANBUL, TURKEY
If I didn't have my phone for a week, I wouldn't be able to live. It's too important to be without. That's what I thought. When I feel like chatting with my friends, I'll use my phone. I even broke up with my last boyfriend using my phone. Without it, I wouldn't be able to know everything that's happening. But this week, I actually enjoyed not having it. I could concentrate better, I wasn't too worried about what everyone was saying or doing and I spent more time actually talking to my friends.

EDUARDO, 46, BUSINESSMAN, MEXICO CITY, MEXICO
I'm on my smartphone all day. If I couldn't use it for a week, I wouldn't be able to take care of my business. It would be a disaster. Well, that's what I thought – but it wasn't. I worked more effectively when I was in the office, I had more time to think about everything and in the evenings, I was a lot more relaxed. I realised that I could put off making decisions until I was in the office. It's really changed how I work and I think the business is actually doing better now.

CARLA, 24, FASHION WRITER, MILAN, ITALY
I write a fashion blog. If I couldn't use my phone, I wouldn't have a job. It's what I do and who I am. When I find out something, I need to pass it on quickly. That's why people read my blog. I tried it for a day, but it was too difficult. I couldn't take any photos of cool people on the streets or quickly add something to my blog when I was out at a party. I just wasn't doing enough. It was horrible.

2 LISTENING

a 10.06 Listen to the conversation and underline the people who said these things.

1 Buying something in a shop is usually more expensive than buying online.
Zuza / *<u>Haluk</u>* / *No one*
2 When you shop online, you can't get what you buy straight away.
Zuza / *Haluk* / *No one*
3 Buying clothes online can be difficult because you can't try them on before you buy them.
Zuza / *Haluk* / *No one*
4 You can't return something that you buy online.
Zuza / *Haluk* / *No one*
5 There are sometimes problems with the delivery of things you buy online.
Zuza / *Haluk* / *No one*
6 If people stopped going to shops, they would all close.
Zuza / *Haluk* / *No one*

b 10.06 Listen to the conversation again and tick (✓) the correct endings to the sentences.

1 Haluk thinks online shopping is better because …
a ☑ you can buy things at any time of the day and it is often cheaper.
b ☐ you don't have to leave your house and it is often cheaper.
c ☐ you don't have to wait more than a few days and it is cheaper.

2 The coat that Haluk bought recently was …
a ☐ damaged in the post.
b ☐ too big for him.
c ☐ the wrong size and colour.

3 The company that sold the coat …
a ☐ has given him an explanation of what happened.
b ☐ has given him a refund.
c ☐ hasn't replied to his email.

4 Haluk buys books online because …
a ☐ he doesn't like going to bookshops.
b ☐ he can find more books online than in the bookshop.
c ☐ the bookshop in his town has closed.

5 Zuza thinks that online shopping …
a ☐ will have an effect on shops in the future.
b ☐ has already had an effect on shops in her town.
c ☐ is more fun than normal shopping.

6 Which of the statements is not true?
a ☐ Zuza hopes that she will meet someone when she is shopping.
b ☐ Zuza thinks that Haluk should stop buying things online.
c ☐ Zuza thinks that Haluk will meet someone while he is at home.

c Write about the advantages and disadvantages of shopping online. Include answers to these questions:

- What have you bought online?
- Why did you buy it online?
- Did you have any problems buying it online?

Review and extension

1 GRAMMAR

Correct the sentences.

1 This table isn't enough big for 20 people.
This table isn't big enough for 20 people.
2 He invited too much people to his party – over 100!
3 If I would have a motorbike, I wouldn't take the bus to work.
4 This morning it was too cold for swim in the sea.
5 I will go on a diet if I were overweight.
6 If Chile would win the World Cup, he would be delighted.

2 VOCABULARY

Correct the sentences.

1 Could you look at my cat while I'm on holiday?
Could you look after my cat while I'm on holiday?
2 Tim isn't here at the moment, but I can pass a message.
3 The restaurant only has a small menu, so the choose of food is very limited.
4 It's sad that Ana and Esteban have broken down after being together for ten years.
5 If you aren't happy with your hotel, you should complaint.
6 She was offered a better job, but she turned it off.

3 WORDPOWER
Multi-word verbs with *on*

Underline the correct words to complete the sentences.

1 He *got* / *<u>tried</u>* / *kept* on the shoes, but they were too big.
2 I can't *go* / *put* / *get* on working so much – I'm exhausted!
3 It was quite dark in the restaurant, so I had to *get* / *carry* / *put* on my glasses to read the menu.
4 I'm not sleeping well because my neighbour's dog *puts* / *keeps* / *tries* on barking all night long.
5 It was a really cold day, so she decided to *put* / *try* / *carry* on her scarf and gloves.
6 Although it started raining, we decided to *put* / *try* / *carry* on playing tennis for another 20 minutes.
7 He stopped playing video games and *tried* / *got* / *put* on with his homework.
8 Although they were dirty, I *kept* / *put* / *went* my shoes on when I went into his house.

REVIEW YOUR PROGRESS

Look again at Review Your Progress on p. 106 of the Student's Book. How well can you do these things now?
3 = very well 2 = well 1 = not so well

I CAN …	
talk about moral dilemmas	☐
describe problems with goods and services	☐
return goods and make complaints	☐
write an apology email.	☐

11A IT'S A ROBOT THAT LOOKS LIKE A HUMAN

1 GRAMMAR Defining relative clauses

a Complete the sentences with *who*, *which* or *where*.

1 Charles Dickens was the English author _who_ wrote *Oliver Twist*.
2 The Louvre is the museum in Paris ________ you can see the famous *Mona Lisa* by Leonardo da Vinci.
3 Last night we watched a TV programme ________ explained the causes of the First World War.
4 When I was on holiday, I met a man ________ worked for the BBC in Manchester.
5 This is the place in New Zealand ________ they made the *The Lord of the Rings* films.
6 Tim Berners-Lee was the scientist ________ invented the World Wide Web in the early 1990s.
7 That's the app ________ counts your steps every day.
8 Near where I work, there's a gym ________ only costs £20 per month.
9 He knows a restaurant near the train station ________ you can have a delicious three-course meal for only £15.
10 Maria's got an aunt in England ________ has been married four times!

b Correct the sentences.

1 There are some nice boots in that shop who cost only £35!
There are some nice boots in that shop which cost only £35!
OR
There are some nice boots in that shop that cost only £35!
2 There's a woman over there which used to work for your company.
____
3 There's a café near me it has 50 different kinds of tea!
____
4 My dad's got a cousin in Houston he works for NASA.
____
5 I know an Italian restaurant in London that you can have chocolate spaghetti!
____
6 I got a new phone who also comes with free music apps.
____
7 That's the cinema which they're showing the new Superman film next week.
____
8 He's just bought a new TV it has amazing picture quality.
____

2 VOCABULARY Compound nouns

a Complete the crossword puzzle.

→ Across

3 I bought my boots at the new s_hoe_ s_hop_ across from the café.
4 *The Invisible Man* is a s______ f______ story.
5 Can you cut me a slice using the b______ knife?
8 Can you read that r______ s______ on the side of the motorway?
11 Mick Jagger from the band The Rolling Stones is a world-famous r______ s______.

↓ Down

1 My keys are on a key r______ so I don't lose them.
2 Can you get me six c______ cups from the cupboard, please?
4 The film *Forrest Gump* was famous for its s______. It had so many great songs.
6 I'm sure I wrote down her telephone number in my a______ book.
7 The street l______ turn on automatically when it starts getting dark.
9 At the end of the day, her eyes are tired from looking at the computer s______.
10 Can you imagine a future with driverless c______? What will people do while they're on the motorway?

3 PRONUNCIATION Word stress: compound nouns

a 11.01 Listen to the compound nouns and underline the main stressed syllable.

1 mountain climbing
2 computer screen
3 science fiction
4 address book
5 bread knife
6 car park
7 coffee cup
8 bookshelf

11B I THINK THEY DISCOVERED IT BY CHANCE

1 GRAMMAR Articles

a Complete the conversation at a tourist office with the correct articles: *a*, *an*, *the* or Ø.

A Good morning. Please take [1]__*a*__ seat. I'll be with you in [2]______ moment … Now, how can I help you?
B Could you help us to find [3]______ hotel in [4]______ London, please?
A Yes, of course. Would you like [5]______ hotel in the city centre?
B Yes, if possible.
A OK, how about [6]______ Grand Hotel? They've got some rooms available.
B Is it near [7]______ underground station?
A Yes, it is. It's about five minutes' walk from [8]______ Marble Arch station. And it's very close to [9]______ Hyde Park. It's one of [10]______ nicest hotels in London.
B Great. Can you ask if they have [11]______ double room for three nights? And can you check [12]______ price?
A Yes, sure. I'm afraid [13]______ hotels in London are really expensive. A lot of [14]______ people think that London's [15]______ most expensive city for [16]______ tourists in [17]______ world.
B Yes, [18]______ hotel that we stayed in last year cost over £200 a night!
A Let's see … A double room is £130 a night.
B OK, that's fine. We'll take it.
A Right, I've booked it for you. When you come out of [19]______ underground station, go along [20]______ Edgware Road for about 200 metres and it's on [21]______ right, opposite [22]______ cinema.
B Brilliant. Thanks very much.

b 11.02 Listen and check.

c Correct the sentences.

1. That film was most exciting thriller I've ever seen.
   That film was the most exciting thriller I've ever seen.
2. In the UK, the police officers don't usually carry guns.
   ____
3. I love the Italian ice cream. It's the best in the world!
   ____
4. They drove to Paris by car and stayed in the lovely hotel near the Eiffel Tower.
   ____
5. France is the most popular country for the tourists in the world.
   ____
6. Doctors in USA are paid much more than nurses.
   ____

2 VOCABULARY Adverbials: luck and chance

a Match 1–8 with a–h to make sentences.

1 [f] I didn't have enough money to pay the taxi driver, but fortunately,
2 [ ] He didn't train very hard for his first marathon, but amazingly,
3 [ ] Look, I didn't break your phone on purpose. I
4 [ ] While they were moving the furniture around, they accidentally
5 [ ] The president was very popular so, as expected,
6 [ ] We got to the airport on time, but unfortunately,
7 [ ] My grandmother fell over again yesterday, but luckily,
8 [ ] I found these old letters from my uncle by chance

a accidentally dropped it while I was getting out of the car.
b he won the election very easily with 75% of the vote.
c while I was fixing the old desk in my aunt's bedroom.
d broke my computer screen.
e our flight to Moscow was delayed because of the storms.
f my friend had ten euros that she lent me.
g he finished it in just under three hours.
h she didn't break her arm this time.

b Underline the correct words to complete the sentences.

1. *Surprisingly* / *<u>As expected</u>*, Real Madrid beat the third division team very easily, winning 6 – 0.
2. *Luckily* / *Unfortunately*, I've lost my front door key, so I can't get into my house.
3. The ruins of the ancient city were discovered completely *by chance* / *on purpose* while the construction company were building the new motorway.
4. *Accidentally* / *Luckily*, it stopped raining in the afternoon, so we were able to take the children to the beach.
5. Sorry, but it was an accident. I didn't do it *on purpose* / *as expected*.
6. *Unfortunately* / *Amazingly*, although he didn't work very hard, he got 95% in his final exam!

3 PRONUNCIATION Word stress: adverbials

a 11.03 Listen to the words and tick (✓) the stressed syllable in each word.

1 accidentally — a [ ] ac b [✓] den
2 on purpose — a [ ] pur b [ ] pose
3 by chance — a [ ] by b [ ] chance
4 unfortunately — a [ ] un b [ ] for
5 luckily — a [ ] luc b [ ] ly
6 surprisingly — a [ ] sur b [ ] pri
7 amazingly — a [ ] ma b [ ] zing
8 fortunately — a [ ] for b [ ] nate
9 as expected — a [ ] ex b [ ] pec

11C EVERYDAY ENGLISH
It's straight ahead

1 USEFUL LANGUAGE Asking for and giving directions in a building

a 11.04 Listen and put the directions in the correct order.

Can you tell me where the Kensington Meeting Room is?
- ☐ Then go up the stairs to the first floor.
- ☐ The Kensington Room is the fourth door on the right.
- 1 Yes, sure. It's on the first floor.
- ☐ Then go down to the end of the corridor.
- ☐ At the top of the stairs, turn left and go down another corridor.
- ☐ Go through that door over there.

Great, thanks.

b 11.04 Listen again and check.

c Put the words in the correct order to make sentences.

1 the stairs / ground floor / the / to / go down .
Go down the stairs to the ground floor.

2 go through / those / and then / doors / down / the corridor .

____

3 down / so, first / to the / go / stairs / the corridor .

____

4 tell / where / the / you / is, please / staff restaurant / me / could ?

____

5 the right / the / down / and it's / the first / on / office / then go / corridor, .

____

6 floor / go / the / to / stairs / the third / up .

____

7 can / check / so, / just / I ?

____

8 I've / OK, / think / that / I / got .

____

9 corridor / the top of / the / go / another / right and / stairs, / turn / down / at .

____

10 the meeting room / is / second / left / on / the / door / the .

____

d 11.05 Listen and check.

2 PRONUNCIATION Sound and spelling: /ɜː/ and /ɔː/

a 11.06 Listen to the words. Tick (✓) the word you hear from each pair.

	/ɜː/	/ɔː/
1	☐ bird	✓ bored
2	☐ fur	☐ four
3	☐ sir	☐ sore
4	☐ shirt	☐ short
5	☐ word	☐ ward
6	☐ earl	☐ all
7	☐ pearl	☐ Paul
8	☐ worm	☐ warm

11D SKILLS FOR WRITING
In my opinion, it's because of the Internet

1 READING

a Read the posts and tick (✓) the correct answer.

a ☐ Bicycles have always been very cheap to buy.
b ☐ Cycling is a popular hobby for a lot of people.
c ☐ Cycling is bad for the environment.
d ☐ Streets with electric lighting were more dangerous.

b Read the posts again. Are the sentences true (*T*) or false (*F*)?

1 ☐ It was cheaper to have a bicycle than to travel on public transport.
2 ☐ Bicycles are not very popular in the developing world.
3 ☐ When a lot of people cycle to work, cities become less polluted.
4 ☐ Gas lighting was invented after electric lighting.
5 ☐ Reading and writing at night were easier with electric lighting.

2 WRITING SKILLS
Expressing results and reasons

a Underline the correct words to complete the sentences.

1 *As a result of* / *As* / *Because* better windows, new houses lose less heat in winter and people spend less money on keeping them warm.
2 In the 1960s, people couldn't afford to go abroad on holiday *because of* / *as* / *as a result of* air travel was so expensive.
3 People didn't use their phones when they were abroad *as a result of* / *because of* / *because* phone calls were so expensive.
4 Computers are much smaller now *as* / *because* / *because of* the invention of the microchip.
5 *As* / *As a result of* / *Because of* you can now travel by train from London to Paris in less than three hours, I won't need to fly anymore.
6 Nowadays, malaria is less common in Africa *as* / *as a result of* / *because* the new vaccination programme.
7 *Because* / *As* / *Because of* the pollution, some cities only allow people to drive their cars on certain days of the month.
8 She decided to buy a tablet *because of* / *because* / *as a result of* it was much easier to carry around than her old laptop.

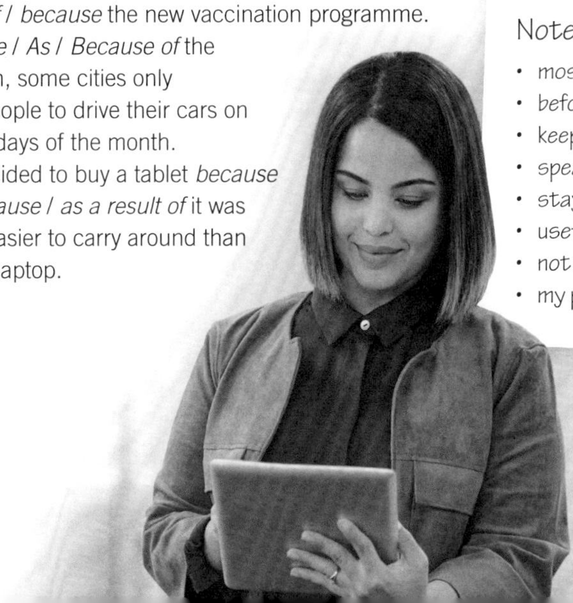

The bicycle was invented in the 19th century. At first, bicycles were very expensive, but at the beginning of the 20th century, they were mass-produced in large factories. As a result of this, they became much cheaper and after that, most people could afford to buy one. Bicycles changed the way people travelled short distances. Because of the bicycle, people who didn't have much money didn't have to travel to work on buses or trains. As a result, they saved money and could get a job further away from where they lived. Today, bicycles are the most important form of transport for people in many countries in the developing world. Cycling is also a very popular sport for many people, as it is a great way to stay fit and healthy. In big cities, a lot of people cycle to work and this helps reduce pollution and protect the environment. Because of this, it seems to me that the bicycle is one of the most important inventions of the last 200 years.

Martin Roberts

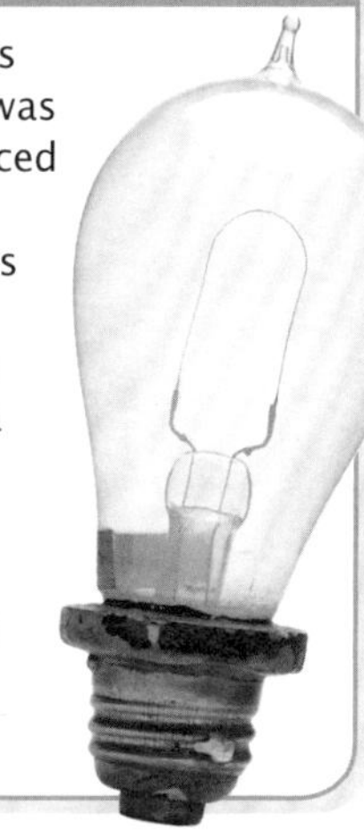

In my opinion, the most important invention is the electric light bulb. The electric light bulb was invented in the 19th century and slowly replaced gas lighting in the streets of big cities and in people's homes. With electric lights, the streets of big cities became safer and, as a result, there was less crime. Also, electric light bulbs improved the lighting in people's houses. As a result, they could do more things when it got dark in the evenings, such as reading books or writing letters. Electric lights have greatly improved the quality of people's lives and it is hard to imagine life without them.

Naomi Stevens

3 WRITING

a Write a post about the invention of mobile phones. Use the notes to help you.

Notes for post about mobile phones

- most important invention = mobile phone
- before: had to be home, office or public phone box
- keep in contact with friends, family, colleagues
- speak wherever you are: street, supermarket, car, train
- stay in touch with children + elderly relatives
- useful if accident or to call the police
- not only calls and texts: also photos, videos, music, Internet, social media
- my phone = my most useful possession: where would I be without it?

UNIT 11
Reading and listening extension

1 READING

a Read the story and complete the sentences.

1 Juliane and her mother took a flight from Lima to Pucallpa.
2 The ____________ was hit by lightning.
3 The plane crashed in the ____________.
4 Juliane found some ____________ to eat.
5 Juliane followed a small ____________ through the forest.
6 Some men found Juliane and took her down the river in a ____________.
7 A small plane flew her to the ____________ in Pucallpa.

b Read the story again. Are the sentences true (*T*) or false (*F*)?

1 ☐ Juliane was the only person who did not die in the crash.
2 ☐ The food that she found belonged to the other passengers.
3 ☐ Juliane was not prepared for life in the rainforest.
4 ☐ There were people in the hut that Juliane found.
5 ☐ The men who found Juliane had a small plane.

c Read the story again. Match 1–6 with a–f to make sentences.

1 The flight which
2 The bone that
3 The lessons that
4 The boat which
5 The men who
6 The hospital where

a found Juliane took her down the river.
b Juliane broke was in her neck.
c Juliane found belonged to the men who helped her.
d Juliane was on crashed in the rainforest.
e Juliane's father taught her helped her survive.
f Juliane was taken was in Pucallpa.

d Imagine you are Juliane. Write a letter to a friend explaining your experience in the forest. Remember to include:

- what happened to you
- how you felt at the time
- how you feel now.

Amazing but True

There are many true stories about people who have been in a plane crash but didn't die, but what happened to Juliane Koepcke is one of the most amazing stories.

Juliane and her parents lived in Peru. On 24 December in 1971, 17-year-old Juliane was on a plane that was flying from Lima to Pucallpa in Peru with her mother, Maria. They were travelling to meet Juliane's father, who was working in Pucallpa.

Unfortunately, the plane never arrived. During the flight, it was hit by lightning and broke up above the rainforest. Juliane fell over 3,000 metres to the ground and landed still in her seat, and amazingly, still alive. Everyone else on board died. Juliane had a broken bone in her neck and cuts on her arms, but surprisingly, she could still walk.

First of all, she tried to find her mother. Unfortunately, she couldn't see her, so she decided to look for some food instead. Luckily, she found some sweets that passengers had taken with them as gifts for their relatives. This was the only food that she found to eat.

Juliane's father was a biologist who had spent a lot of time in the rainforests in Peru with his family. Fortunately, he had taught Juliane some important lessons in how to stay alive. The skills that she had learnt helped her in the rainforest. When she found a small river, she knew that if she followed it, it would take her to a village. It also gave her fresh water to drink and a natural path through the forest.

She walked and swam for nine days until she found an empty hut made of wood. By chance, she also found a boat. Juliane wanted to leave but she didn't want to take the boat because it wasn't hers. So she waited. Luckily, hours later the men who used the hut came back and found Juliane. They helped look after her. The following day, they took her in the boat down the river to a place where there was a small plane, which took her to the hospital in Pucallpa. No one really knows why Juliane lived and everyone else died on the flight, but everyone agrees that it is an amazing story.

2 LISTENING

a 11.07 Listen to the conversation. Number the events in the correct order.

- ☐ The police arrived.
- ☐ The car with one man inside drove into the cash machine.
- ☐ The men drove the car into something in the street.
- ☐ The men ran away into a park.
- ☐ The men took some money from the machine.
- ☐ The men tried to break open the cash machine.
- [1] A car with two men inside drove into the cash machine very fast.

b 11.07 Listen to the conversation again and tick (✓) the correct answers.

1 Where was Margaret Edwards when the vehicle crashed into the cash machine?
  a ☐ in the bedroom
  b ☐ in the bathroom
  c ☑ in another room

2 At first, Margaret thought the crash was …
  a ☐ an accident.
  b ☐ amazing.
  c ☐ done on purpose.

3 What did the men use to try and break open the machine?
  a ☐ something they found in the street
  b ☐ something they were wearing
  c ☐ something that was in the car

4 One of the men …
  a ☐ was wearing dark glasses.
  b ☐ looked like a baseball player.
  c ☐ was much older than the other man.

5 What happened when they opened the cash machine?
  a ☐ They were able to take a lot of money.
  b ☐ The police came.
  c ☐ The men decided to run away.

6 Why didn't the men drive away?
  a ☐ They didn't have the key to the car.
  b ☐ The car was damaged.
  c ☐ The police stopped them.

c Write about a surprising or amazing thing you may have seen. Remember to include:

- what you saw
- what happened
- how you felt.

Review and extension

1 GRAMMAR

Correct the sentences.

1 *Rocky* was the film what Sylvester Stallone made in 1976.
  Rocky was the film that Sylvester Stallone made in 1976.
2 Sorry, I can't talk to you at the moment because I'm at the work.
3 Generally speaking, most the men like watching sport on TV.
4 Modern Living is the shop who I bought my leather sofa.
5 Look! That's a man who stole my wallet!
6 John F Kennedy was the American president which was assassinated in Dallas in 1963.

2 VOCABULARY

Correct the sentences.

1 They're having a sale at the shoes shop next to the cinema.
  They're having a sale at the shoe shop next to the cinema.
2 I think I wrote his phone number in my book address.
3 Surprisedly, it tasted a bit like chicken.
4 I'm afraid of heights, so I don't want to go rockclimbing.
5 He opened the car's door without looking and hit an old man on a bicycle.
6 I'm sorry I broke your cup of coffee – it was an accident.

3 WORDPOWER Preposition + noun

Match 1–6 with a–f to make sentences.

1 [f] Their plane didn't leave on
2 ☐ My parents are still in
3 ☐ I didn't break your glasses on
4 ☐ All of the bank robbers are now in
5 ☐ There are a lot of cheap bikes for
6 ☐ Next time you come to town, tell me in

a love with each other after 30 years of marriage.
b sale on this website. You could get one for Sam's birthday.
c advance so I can book some theatre tickets.
d prison, apart from the one who escaped.
e purpose. I sat on them by mistake.
f time. It was 30 minutes late.

REVIEW YOUR PROGRESS

Look again at Review Your Progress on p. 116 of the Student's Book. How well can you do these things now?
3 = very well 2 = well 1 = not so well

I CAN …	
explain what technology does	☐
talk about discoveries	☐
ask for and give directions in a building	☐
write a post expressing an opinion.	☐

12A I HAD ALWAYS THOUGHT THEY WERE DANGEROUS

1 VOCABULARY Animals

a Complete the crossword puzzle.

→ Across

3 This insect bites humans and drinks their blood. mosquito

5 This animal lives in deserts and can travel long distances without food or water. ________

6 This insect produces honey. ________

7 This bird is large, very colourful, and can learn to 'talk' by copying what someone says to it. ________

↓ Down

1 This animal has eight legs and makes webs to catch small flies. One of the biggest kinds is the tarantula. ________

2 This animal is the largest kind of monkey in the world. ________

4 The blue ________ is the biggest animal on the planet.

8 This is the largest animal of the cat family and is orange with black stripes. ________

2 GRAMMAR Past perfect

a Complete the sentences with the past perfect forms of the verbs in the box.

steal work get up miss stop ~~leave~~ begin finish

1 By the time we got to the station, my sister's train had already left.

2 When my grandmother called, I ________ just ________ doing my homework.

3 He ________ really hard at school all year, so he got excellent marks in his exams.

4 Anthony arrived late for school this morning because he ________ late.

5 When they got to the cinema, the film ________ just ________.

6 When he got back from holiday, he found that someone ________ his car.

7 We had to take a taxi home from the train station because we ________ the last bus.

8 The two men ________ arguing by the time the police arrived.

b Complete the text with the past simple or past perfect forms of the verbs in brackets.

We [1] had (have) a terrible journey on the way from London to Barcelona. The problems [2] ________ (begin) when we [3] ________ (leave) the hotel at 6:30 in the morning. There [4] ________ (be) a huge traffic jam on the motorway because two lorries [5] ________ (crash) and the road [6] ________ (be) completely blocked.

By the time we [7] ________ (reach) the airport, we [8] ________ (miss) our flight. It [9] ________ (take) off five minutes before we [10] ________ (arrive) at the check-in desk. We [11] ________ (try) to buy some tickets for the next flight to Barcelona, but they [12] ________ (sell) out. In the end, we [13] ________ (buy) tickets for a flight at 7 pm and [14] ________ (spend) the whole day at the airport.

We [15] ________ (land) in Barcelona at 9:45 pm, but we [16] ________ (not collect) our suitcases from the arrivals hall until 11 o'clock because there [17] ________ (be) a baggage handlers' strike that day. By the time our taxi driver [18] ________ (find) our hotel, the restaurant [19] ________ (close), so we [20] ________ (go) straight to bed without having dinner.

3 PRONUNCIATION Sound and spelling: /ʌ/, /ɔː/ and /əʊ/

a 12.01 Look at the words and listen to the pronunciation of the letters in **bold**. Complete the table with the words in the box.

~~br**ough**t~~ c**o**me d**o**ne f**a**llen kn**ow**n
sp**o**ken r**u**n t**au**ght w**o**ken w**o**n

Sound 1 /ʌ/ (e.g., *dr**u**nk*)	Sound 2 /ɔː/ (e.g., *b**ough**t*)	Sound 3 /əʊ/ (e.g., *ch**o**sen*)
	brought	

12B HE SAID I WAS SELFISH!

1 GRAMMAR Reported speech

a Underline the correct words to complete the sentences.

1 Matthew said, 'I want to play football with my friends.'
He *told me / said me / told* that *we want / I wanted / he wanted* to play football with *my / his / your* friends.

2 Naomi said, 'I'll help you with the washing up.'
She *told / said / said me* that *she will / I would / she would* help *me / her / you* with the washing up.

3 Angela said, 'My mum's watching a film with my little brother.'
She *told / told me / said me* that *my / his / her* mum *had watched / was watching / watching* a film with *her / his / my* little brother.

4 David said, 'We went to the park with some friends from our school.'
He *said / told / said me* that *they've been / they'd been / we've been* to the park with some friends from *our / her / their* school.

5 James said, 'Andy, my dad can't take us to the zoo on Saturday.'
He *said me / told him / said him* that *my / her / his* dad *couldn't / could / didn't can* take *us / them / me* to the zoo on Saturday.

6 Josh said, 'I think that we'll go to the beach with our cousins after lunch.'
He *told / told us / said us* that he *is thinking / thought / had thought* that *we will go / he would go / they would go* to the beach with *my / their / her* cousins after lunch.

7 She said, 'I've already done all of my homework.'
She *said / told / said me* that *she already did / I've already done / she'd already done* all of *my / his / her* homework.

8 Adam said, 'My sister isn't going to come to my birthday party!'
He *told / told us / said us* that *my / her / his* sister *isn't going to / wasn't going to / not going to* come to *his / her / our* birthday party.

b Read the direct speech sentences. Use reported speech to report what the speaker said. Make any necessary changes to the highlighted words.

1 'I'm waiting for my bus to come.'
She said she was waiting for her bus to come. OR
She said that she was waiting for her bus to come.

2 'I'll invite you and your brother to my house for dinner next week.'
He told me …

3 'You can use my computer to do your homework.'
She told James …

4 'The traffic was really bad, so we missed the 5:15 train.'
He said …

5 'We're going to buy you a lovely present for your birthday.'
She told me …

6 'I've tried calling my friend, but she didn't answer, so I think she's away on holiday.'
He said …

2 VOCABULARY Personality adjectives

a Complete the crossword puzzle.

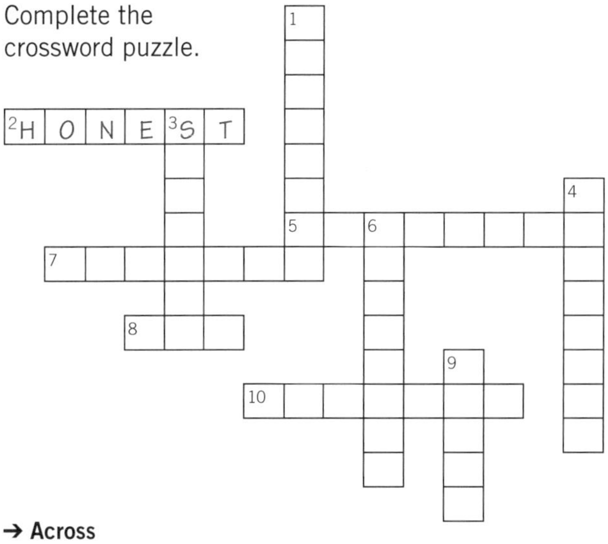

→ Across

2 He's so honest! When a shop assistant gave him too much change yesterday, he didn't keep it – he told her she'd made a mistake.

5 She's extremely ________ – she has a lot of friends and she loves meeting new people.

7 You know, I've never seen Jim laugh and he rarely smiles – he's always so ________.

8 She's really ________ – she hates having to talk to people she doesn't know at parties.

10 He's a very ________ person – he worries about everything.

↓ Down

1 You're so ________! That's the second time you've lost your keys this month.

3 You're so ________ – why should we always do what you want to do? Why can't you think about other people for a change?

4 She's a very ________ person. Although she hasn't got much money, she bought all her friends dinner when it was her birthday.

6 He's a very ________ person – he writes poems and short stories and loves painting.

9 Mike's a really ________ guy – he's always telling us jokes and making us laugh.

12C EVERYDAY ENGLISH

I'm pretty sure it's Japanese

1 USEFUL LANGUAGE Agreeing and disagreeing

a Match 1–8 with a–h to make exchanges.

1 [g] I believe yoga is a great way to relax before you go to bed.
2 [ ] I think Brazil have the best football team in the world.
3 [ ] In my opinion, Venice is a more attractive city than Florence.
4 [ ] This is a nicer cinema than the one we went to last week.
5 [ ] Barcelona is the biggest city in Spain.
6 [ ] I think Leonardo DiCaprio is a better actor than Brad Pitt.
7 [ ] In my opinion, Italian coffee is better than French coffee.
8 [ ] I think the weather in the UK in winter is much better than in Germany.

a I don't think so. I think there are more people in Madrid, actually.
b Definitely. He was brilliant in *Once Upon A Time in Hollywood*.
c I agree. The seats are very comfortable and the screen is wider.
d I'm not sure about that. I think that Argentina will beat them in the final.
e Definitely. It's such a beautiful place to visit. I love it!
f I'm afraid I don't agree. It rains so much here in January and February. I can't stand it!
g You're absolutely right. I do yoga every night.
h I'm sorry, but how do you know? You don't drink coffee!

b 12.02 Listen and check.

c Underline the correct words to complete the exchanges.

1 **A** I think the Amazon is the longest river in the world.
B *Definitely.* / *I don't think so.* / *That's true.* Actually, I think the Nile is longer than the Amazon.

2 **A** I think Swiss chocolate is much nicer than British chocolate.
B *You're absolutely right.* / *Oh, please.* / *I'm not sure about that.* It's possibly the best in the world.

3 **A** Russian is a harder language to learn than Spanish.
B *Oh, please.* / *I don't think so.* / *Definitely.* In my opinion, Spanish is one of the easiest languages to learn.

4 **A** Everybody should retire when they reach 60.
B *That's right.* / *Oh, please.* / *Exactly.* That's way too early! Older people have so much experience which they can pass on to their younger colleagues.

5 **A** Tablets are so much more practical than laptops.
B *I'm sorry, but I don't agree.* / *I'm afraid you're wrong.* / *That's true.* They're much lighter and easier to carry.

6 **A** His last film was brilliant!
B *I'm not sure about that.* / *You're right.* / *I don't think so.* It's the best film he's made so far.

d 12.03 Listen and check.

2 PRONUNCIATION Main stress: contrastive

a 12.04 Listen to the exchanges and tick (✓) the stressed word in each of B's responses.

	Stressed word
1 **A** Antonio Banderas is a Mexican actor. **B** Er, he's actually a Spanish actor.	Spanish ✓ actor
2 **A** French food's the best in the world. **B** Well, actually, I think Italian food is the best.	Italian food
3 **A** I like the American English accent. **B** Do you? I prefer British English, actually.	British English
4 **A** New York's the best place to live in the USA. **B** Actually, I think San Francisco's the best place.	San Francisco best
5 **A** I think Chelsea will win the Champions League this year. **B** No way! Barcelona will win it this year.	Barcelona win
6 **A** Baseball is the most popular sport in the USA. **B** I'm sorry, but I think American football is the most popular sport.	American football sport

12D SKILLS FOR WRITING

A few hours later, they started baking again

1 READING

a Read the text and tick (✓) the correct answer.

a ☐ The old lady lost her handbag in the park.
b ☐ The thief gave the handbag back to the old lady.
c ☐ The police officers thought Tom had stolen a handbag.
d ☐ Tom stopped a man who had taken a lady's handbag.

b Read the text again. Are the sentences true (*T*) or false (*F*)?

1 ☐ Tom was walking across the park with Brian when he heard the old lady.
2 ☐ The young man couldn't escape because Tom was sitting on him.
3 ☐ Both police officers asked Tom to explain what had happened.
4 ☐ Tom didn't want to accept the old lady's money at first.
5 ☐ The old lady didn't have much money.

2 WRITING SKILLS
Linkers: past time

a Underline the correct words to complete the sentences.

1 *As soon as* / *After a while* the police arrived, the man started running down the street.
2 He saw the strange man with the black dog at 7:30 in the morning. *By morning* / *Later that day*, he saw him again, but this time without his dog.
3 They said goodnight and went back to their hotel to sleep. *As soon as* / *The following morning*, they caught the train to Paris.
4 It started to snow late last night. *By morning*, / *After a while*, when we woke up, the entire city was covered in snow!
5 The sky was covered in dark clouds. *A few hours later* / *Later that year*, it started to rain very heavily.

Local Hero

One hot day last July, Tom was walking home from university after playing in a rugby match. He had just said goodbye to his best friend, Brian, and was walking across the park near his house. Suddenly, he heard someone shouting, 'Stop, thief!' He turned round and saw a little old lady. She was pointing at a young man of about 20 who was running towards him. 'He's stolen my handbag!' she shouted. The thief was coming towards Tom and the old lady shouted to him, 'Hey, you! Stop him!' A few seconds later, Tom threw himself at the young man and the thief fell over on the path. Tom immediately sat on the thief's back so he couldn't escape. A few minutes later Tom heard a siren and saw the flashing blue light of a police car. The old lady had called the police on her phone and, luckily, a police car had been near the park at the time.

Two police officers got out of the car quickly and ran towards Tom and the thief as fast as they could. As soon as they got to Tom, they immediately arrested the young man. While one of them took him to the police car, the other one started asking Tom and the old lady some questions about what had happened. Tom gave the old lady her handbag. Fortunately, everything was still inside it. The old lady thanked Tom and asked him for his telephone number. She explained that she had to leave because she was going to visit a friend in hospital. When the old lady had gone, Tom told the police officer what had happened and he wrote everything down in his notebook. Finally, he gave the police officer his phone number and went home.

The following day, the old lady called Tom. She thanked him again and invited him to her house. She said that she wanted to give him a reward. Later that week, Tom went to visit the old lady at her house. She lived in a big house near the park and there was a Rolls-Royce in front of it. While they were talking, she made him a cup of tea and gave him some delicious chocolate cake. Then, just as he was standing up to leave, she opened her handbag and gave him £500. Tom told her that he didn't want to take it, but she insisted: 'Please take it. I've got plenty of money and I'd really like to thank you for being so brave.' In the end, Tom agreed to take it. By the end of the week, he had used the money to buy a new laptop.

3 WRITING

a David went on a climbing trip in Scotland last year. Write a story about what happened. Use the time expressions in the box and the notes to help you.

about an hour later	ten minutes later	after a while	later that day
as soon as suddenly	by the following day	soon	last year when

Notes on accident during climbing trip

- Scotland + 3 friends
- accident – top of a mountain? eating sandwiches?
- weather changed – heavy snow – only see 20 metres
- started climbing down path: next village (spend the night?)
- snow: getting deeper?
- all confident climbers: no problems?
- shout from behind me: Anthony lying on the ground (fallen over a rock?)
- leg hurting badly: broken?
- call for help? Phone: emergency services
- mountain rescue team (helicopter)
- arrived hospital
- leg not badly broken: no need to operate and he was able to leave the hospital the following day – all felt very relieved

UNIT 12
Reading and listening extension

We Bought a Zoo

In March 2005, Benjamin Mee received a letter from his sister. Inside was an advertisement for a house that was for sale. It was a house with a zoo full of animals in its garden.

Earlier that year, Benjamin's father had died and his mother was living alone in a large house in London, which she was trying to sell for £1.2 million, the same price as the zoo. Benjamin, who was living in France with his wife and two children, thought that it would be wonderful for his family to sell his mother's house and buy the zoo so that they could all live together and take care of each other. He knew that his father, a sensible man, would not have agreed. But Benjamin was thinking of the future.

Surprisingly, his family agreed. Benjamin's mother was very generous and happy to buy the zoo after selling her house. The year before, she had spent a day at a zoo helping the zookeepers and had really enjoyed taking care of the animals. Benjamin's wife was more anxious. She was very ill and didn't want to change her life, but Benjamin said that it would help her and the children think about something else.

Unfortunately, buying the zoo was quite difficult, but Benjamin was patient and confident, and after a year of trying, in October 2006, they did it. But four days after the family moved into the zoo, there was a disaster. A jaguar, a large spotted cat, had escaped after a zookeeper had forgotten to close a door. The family also needed over £500,000 for repairs before they could open the zoo. Then while they were doing the repairs, Benjamin's wife died.

On 7 July, 2007, the zoo opened, and the first visitors came to see the animals. There were tigers, bears, monkeys, parrots, snakes and spiders, and a lot of other animals. People loved the zoo and loved what Benjamin, his children, who were always sociable and friendly with visitors, and his family had done.

In 2008, he wrote a book called *We Bought a Zoo*, which became very popular. A Hollywood producer read the story and decided to make a film about it. In 2012, the film was released, and the money Benjamin earned from it helped pay the bills and keep the zoo open.

If you'd like to visit the zoo that Benjamin's family bought, it's called the Dartmoor Zoological Gardens, in southwest England.

1 READING

a Read the magazine article above. Put the events in the correct order.

- [ ] Benjamin and his family buy the zoo.
- [1] Benjamin's mother spends a day at a zoo.
- [ ] The zoo opens.
- [ ] Benjamin's father dies.
- [ ] A Hollywood film is made about the zoo.
- [ ] Benjamin receives a letter from his sister.

b Read the magazine article again. Match the adjectives and the descriptions with the people. Complete the table with the words in the boxes.

Adjectives	Descriptions
anxious	friendly with people
generous	gave a lot of money to buy something
~~patient~~	~~waited a year to do something~~
sociable	was worried about changing something

	Adjective	Description
1 Benjamin	*patient*	*waited a year to do something*
2 Benjamin's wife		
3 Benjamin's mother		
4 Benjamin's children		

c Read the magazine article again. Tick (✓) the correct responses.

1 Why did Benjamin want to buy the zoo?
   a [ ] He had always wanted to work with animals.
   b [✓] He wanted to bring his family closer at a difficult time.
   c [ ] His mother was a zookeeper.

2 How did the jaguar escape?
   a [ ] The zookeeper hadn't done something that was important.
   b [ ] The zoo needed to be repaired.
   c [ ] A visitor opened the door.

3 Benjamin's wife died …
   a [ ] before Benjamin bought the zoo.
   b [ ] before the zoo opened.
   c [ ] when the zoo opened.

4 How did the Hollywood film help Benjamin and the zoo?
   a [ ] A lot of people visited the zoo after they saw the film.
   b [ ] Benjamin wrote a book about it.
   c [ ] The money he got helped run the zoo.

d Write a paragraph about a trip that you have recently been on. Remember to include:

- where you went
- what you did
- what you had to prepare before you went
- what you thought of the trip.

2 LISTENING

a ▶ 12.05 Listen to the conversation. Put the events in the correct order.

[ ] Brad goes back to the factory to collect the jewellery.
[ ] Brad leaves the hostel with 10 dollars.
[1] Brad meets two brothers in a tea house.
[ ] Brad runs away and gets in a taxi.
[ ] The brothers make Brad 30 necklaces.
[ ] The brothers take Brad to a cash machine.
[ ] The three men go sightseeing together.
[ ] The two brothers take Brad to their jewellery factory.

b ▶ 12.05 Listen to the conversation again and read the sentences in direct speech. They are from Brad's story, but he uses reported speech. Tick (✓) the correct answers.

1 'We can take you to see some tigers tomorrow.'
Who said this?
a [ ] Brad b [ ] Jay c [✓] Viki

2 'I'll buy a small piece.'
Who said this?
a [ ] Brad b [ ] Jay c [ ] Viki

3 'It will be ready tomorrow.'
What will be ready tomorrow?
a [ ] the money
b [ ] the jewellery
c [ ] the hostel

4 'This is what you asked for yesterday.'
What is *this*?
a [ ] a small piece of jewellery
b [ ] 30 necklaces
c [ ] the money

5 'You will have to pay 100 dollars.'
What for?
a [ ] for the 30 necklaces
b [ ] for the small piece of jewellery
c [ ] for sightseeing

6 'I will take you to a cash machine.'
Who said this?
a [ ] Brad b [ ] Jay c [ ] Viki

c Write about a good or bad experience you've had on holiday. Remember to include:

- where you were
- what happened
- who you met.

Review and extension

1 GRAMMAR

Correct the sentences.

1 By the time we got to his house, the party finished.
By the time we got to his house, the party had finished.
2 I said her that she couldn't go to the beach by herself.
3 He told me that my mother has called earlier that day.
4 We told that her father wouldn't buy her a new computer.
5 Tom never rode a camel before, so he was quite nervous.
6 Our train has already left when we finally arrived at the station.

2 VOCABULARY

Correct the sentences.

1 I had a great time at your party on Saturday. It was really funny.
I had a great time at your party on Saturday. It was really fun.
2 She's a really onest person. If shop assistants give her too much change, she always tells them.
3 He's very easy going. I'm sure he won't mind if you bring your friend with you when you go to his house for dinner.
4 I'm not a very confidant person. For example, I don't like speaking when I'm in a meeting with a large group of people.
5 Teachers have to learn to be patent with their students because sometimes they don't learn things immediately.
6 Why are you always so carless? You've already lost your phone twice this year!

3 WORDPOWER *age*

Underline the correct words to complete the sentences.

1 My father's 48 this year, so he's definitely *of middle age / middle aged / in the middle of age.*
2 *At your age / In your age / On your age*, I was working 12 hours a day in a factory.
3 It's really important for young people to save money for their *older age / old age / third age.*
4 They're sisters who are only 18 months *different of age / apart in age / age difference.*
5 I learnt to read *at an early age / of early age / at young age* – I could read when I was only three.
6 He's *near my age / old like me / about my age* – we both went to university at the same time.

REVIEW YOUR PROGRESS

Look again at Review Your Progress on p. 126 of the Student's Book. How well can you do these things now?
3 = very well 2 = well 1 = not so well

I CAN ...	
tell a story	[ ]
talk about family relationships	[ ]
agree and disagree in discussions	[ ]
write a short story.	[ ]

UNIT 1: Communicating

1a Where do you usually meet new people?

a Watch video 1a and underline the correct words to complete the sentences.

1 Helen usually meets new people *through friends* / *at parties* / *on trains or buses.*
2 Ian usually meets new people *through cycling* / *through friends* / *at parties.*
3 Carla usually meets new people *at language classes or dance classes* / *through friends* / *through cycling.*
4 Jen usually meets new people *on trains or buses* / *at parties* / *at language classes or dance classes.*
5 Maria usually meets new people *on trains or buses* / *through cycling* / *through friends.*

1b What's a good first question to ask someone?

b Watch video 1b. Match 1–4 with a–d to make sentences.

1 [b] Helen's first question is usually about
2 [ ] Carla's first question is usually about
3 [ ] Jen's first question is usually about
4 [ ] Maria's first question is usually about

a the weather or where the person is from.
b something in the news or the weather.
c the person's hobbies.
d the person's free-time activities.

1c How do you keep in touch with your family?

c Watch video 1c and tick (✓) the correct answers.

1 Helen uses Skype or email to keep in touch with …
a [ ] her parents.
b [ ] her brother.
c [✓] her son.

2 Ian usually communicates with his family …
a [ ] by phone.
b [ ] by letter.
c [ ] on Facebook.

3 Maria keeps in touch with her family …
a [ ] by letter.
b [ ] on the Internet.
c [ ] by text.

4 Carla contacts her family …
a [ ] on her phone.
b [ ] in person.
c [ ] on her laptop.

5 Jen keeps in touch with her family by …
a [ ] seeing them face to face.
b [ ] sending them texts.
c [ ] phoning them.

6 Maria communicates with her family …
a [ ] face to face.
b [ ] by phone.
c [ ] on Facebook.

UNIT 2: Travel

2a What was your last holiday like?

a Watch video 2a and tick (✓) the correct answers.

1 Jenny travelled around the USA by …
a [ ] car.
b [ ] train.
c [✓] coach.

2 John spent his last holiday in …
a [ ] London and Wales.
b [ ] London and Scotland.
c [ ] Scotland and Ireland.

3 Suzanne went to Mexico for …
a [ ] one week.
b [ ] two weeks.
c [ ] three weeks.

4 For Rebecca's last holiday, she went to …
a [ ] the USA.
b [ ] South America.
c [ ] Scotland.

2b Did you do any sightseeing?

b Watch video 2b and tick (✓) the correct answers.

1 Jenny visited …
a [ ] New York and Boston.
b [ ] Chicago and Los Angeles.
c [✓] San Francisco and Las Vegas.

2 John visited …
a [ ] Big Ben and the Houses of Parliament.
b [ ] Buckingham Palace and Westminster Abbey.
c [ ] the Tower of London and Big Ben.

3 When she was in Mexico, Suzanne …
a [ ] did lots of sightseeing.
b [ ] didn't do any sightseeing.
c [ ] spent most of her time relaxing.

4 When she went to Chicago, Rebecca …
a [ ] went on a bus tour.
b [ ] saw the Hollywood sign.
c [ ] didn't do much sightseeing.

2c Did you bring back any souvenirs?

c Watch video 2c. Match 1–4 with a–d to make sentences.

1 [d] When she went on her last holiday, Jenny
2 [ ] When he went on his last holiday, John
3 [ ] When she went on her last holiday, Suzanne
4 [ ] When she went on her last holiday, Rebecca

a didn't bring back any souvenirs.
b brought back lots of souvenirs.
c brought back some presents for his daughters.
d brought back a 'dream catcher'.

UNIT 3: Money

3a What three things have you bought recently?

a Watch video 3a. Complete the sentences with the names in the box.

Darren	Colin	~~Lauren~~	Carolyn

1 ___Lauren___ recently bought some food, some shoes and a magazine.
2 ____________ recently bought some shoes, a T-shirt and a holiday.
3 ____________ recently bought a dress, a fancy-dress costume and some bike lights.
4 ____________ recently bought some spaghetti, some tomato sauce and a house.

3b Is there anything you've bought in the last year but haven't used yet?

b Watch video 3b and underline the correct words to complete the sentences.

1 Lauren has some *shirts* / *shoes* / *jeans* she's never worn.
2 Carolyn bought a black dress *six months ago* / *last weekend* / *a year ago* in the sales.
3 Colin *never buys* / *doesn't usually buy* / *often buys* things he doesn't need.

3c What are good ways to raise money for charity?

c Watch video 3c. Match the ideas for raising money 1–4 with the people who mentioned the ideas a–d.

1 [d] My favourite way of making money is to sell cakes to people.
2 [ ] A friend of mine raised money by cycling across Morocco.
3 [ ] You can cycle from London to Brighton to raise money for charity.
4 [ ] You can cut your hair really short to raise money for charity.

a Lauren
b Darren
c Colin
d Carolyn

UNIT 4: Social Life

4a What's the best party you've ever been to?

a Watch video 4a and tick (✓) the correct answers.

1 The best party Seb's ever been to was …
 a [ ] his brother's birthday party.
 b [ ] his school's Christmas party.
 c [✓] his friend's birthday party.
2 The best party Lucy's ever been to was …
 a [ ] her best friend's birthday party.
 b [ ] her own party.
 c [ ] her father's 50th birthday party.
3 The best party Wiktoria's ever been to was …
 a [ ] Simon's leaving party.
 b [ ] Simon's birthday party.
 c [ ] Simon's end-of-year party.
4 One of Solyman's favourite parties was when …
 a [ ] he was about 6.
 b [ ] he was about 16.
 c [ ] he was a student.

4b What do you usually do to celebrate your birthday?

b Watch video 4b and underline the correct words to complete the sentences.

1 Last year Seb *had a party* / *did two special activities* / *went to a restaurant* with his friends.
2 Lucy usually has a *big party with all her friends* / *meal with her friends* / *meal with her family*.
3 Wiktoria usually has a *barbecue with her friends* / *barbecue with her family* / *party with her friends*.
4 Solyman *doesn't celebrate* / *always celebrates* / *sometimes celebrates* his birthday.

4c What are your plans for the weekend?

c Watch video 4c. Match 1–4 with a–d to make sentences.

1 [b] This weekend Seb is
2 [ ] This weekend Lucy is
3 [ ] This weekend Wiktoria is
4 [ ] This weekend Solyman is

a doing some gardening.
b watching films with some friends.
c getting ready to go on holiday.
d going to London.

UNIT 5: Work

5a Do you work?

a Watch video 5a and tick (✓) the correct answers

1 Jen is a teacher of ___________.
- a ☐ English
- b ☐ German
- c ☑ Russian

2 Christian shows ___________ around Cambridge colleges.
- a ☐ teachers
- b ☐ tourists
- c ☐ students

3 Precious is working with children at a ___________ school.
- a ☐ language
- b ☐ Sunday
- c ☐ summer

4 Helen visits ___________ and clients two or three days a week.
- a ☐ hospitals
- b ☐ hostels
- c ☐ hotels

5b What qualifications or abilities are necessary for your job?

b Watch video 5b and underline the correct words to complete the sentences.

1 In Jen's job you need to be able to *write* / *speak* / *understand* the language you're teaching.
2 In Christian's job you have to be good at *listening to* / *working with* / *talking to* people.
3 In Precious's job you need to be very *friendly* / *funny* / *creative*.
4 People who do Helen's job often have a background in *engineering* / *computing* / *science*.

5c What do you think makes people happy at work?

c Watch video 5c. Match 1–4 with a–d to make sentences.

1 [b] Jen thinks that people like their jobs if
2 ☐ Christian thinks that people like their jobs if
3 ☐ Precious thinks that people like their jobs if
4 ☐ Helen thinks that people like their jobs if

a they get on well with their colleagues.
b there is a nice atmosphere at work.
c they are doing something they really enjoy.
d they get personal satisfaction from their work.

UNIT 6: Problems and Advice

6a When you have a problem, who do you prefer to talk to about it?

a Watch video 6a. Match 1–4 with a–d to make sentences.

1 [d] When Mark has a problem, he prefers to discuss it with his
2 ☐ When Laurence has a problem, he prefers to discuss it with his
3 ☐ When Maibritt has a problem, she prefers to discuss it with her
4 ☐ When Colin has a problem, he prefers to discuss it with his

a husband, sister or friends.
b dad, girlfriend or mum.
c girlfriend or friends.
d best friend.

6b What advice would you give to a student who is worried about exams?

b Watch video 6b. Complete the sentences with the names in the box.

Maibritt	Mark	Colin	~~Laurence~~

1 _Laurence_ would tell the student not to get too worried about the exam.
2 ___________ would tell the student not to panic because it's just an exam.
3 ___________ would tell the student the exam isn't as important as it seems.
4 ___________ would tell the student to relax and do their best.

6c What advice would you give to someone who can't sleep?

c Watch video 6c and tick (✓) the correct answers.

1 Maibritt thinks it's a good idea to read a ___________ before you go to sleep.
- a ☐ magazine
- b ☑ book
- c ☐ newspaper

2 Colin thinks you should get plenty of exercise in the ___________.
- a ☐ morning
- b ☐ afternoon
- c ☐ evening

3 Laurence thinks you shouldn't ___________ before you go to sleep.
- a ☐ look at your phone
- b ☐ watch TV
- c ☐ play computer games

4 Mark thinks you should drink ___________ before you go to sleep.
- a ☐ coffee
- b ☐ tea
- c ☐ milk

UNIT 7: Changes

7a Which life events do you think change people the most?

a Watch video 7a. Match 1–3 with a–c to make sentences.

1 [c] Laurence thinks that people change when they
2 [ ] Darren thinks that people change when they
3 [ ] Peter thinks that people change when they

a get married or have children.
b do something new and exciting for the first time.
c go to university or start a new job.

7b How have you changed in the past five years?

b Watch video 7b. Complete the sentences with the names in the box.

Peter	Laurence	Darren

1 ____________ thinks that now he is very careful about how he spends his time.
2 ____________ thinks that he is more grown up now.
3 ____________ thinks that has learnt a lot about himself.

7c Do you think people in this country are healthier now than they were twenty years ago?

c Watch video 7c and tick (✓) the correct answers.

1 Laurence thinks that when you go out …
  a [ ] it's hard to eat healthy food.
  b [ ] it's better to go to a fast-food restaurant.
  c [ ] it's easy to eat healthy food.

2 Peter thinks that most people …
  a [ ] are very fit and healthy.
  b [ ] are quite fit and healthy.
  c [ ] don't get much exercise.

3 Darren thinks that in general people …
  a [ ] smoke more than before.
  b [ ] smoke less than before.
  c [ ] are less healthy than before.

UNIT 8: Culture

8a Is there a book you've liked since you read it at school?

a Watch video 8a and tick (✓) the correct answers.

1 Stephen ____________.
  a [ ] reads more now than when he was at school
  b [✓] reads less now than when he was at school
  c [ ] has always read a lot of books

2 Malachi has read the Steinbeck novel ____________ since he left school.
  a [ ] once
  b [ ] a few times
  c [ ] five times

3 Sammy ____________.
  a [ ] enjoyed reading some of Shakespeare's plays
  b [ ] didn't enjoy reading Shakespeare's plays
  c [ ] can't remember any of the books he studied at school

8b Is there a sport or activity you've tried but didn't like?

b Watch video 8b. Match 1–4 with a–d to make sentences.

1 [c] Sammy
2 [ ] Stephen
3 [ ] Babs
4 [ ] Malachi

a wasn't very good at basketball because he was very short when he was young.
b has enjoyed all the sports she's tried.
c didn't like rugby because he was quite small when he was younger.
d enjoys doing all sports because he's very competitive.

8c Can you recommend a good film?

c Watch video 8c and tick (✓) the correct answers.

1 Sammy liked *Catch Me If You Can* because …
  a [ ] it was very exciting to watch.
  b [✓] the actors were very good.
  c [ ] it was very funny.

2 Stephen likes watching films because …
  a [ ] books take a long time to read.
  b [ ] they only last for two hours.
  c [ ] you can escape from your daily life.

3 Babs likes *Singing in the Rain* because of …
  a [ ] the acting.
  b [ ] the music.
  c [ ] the photography.

4 Malachi has watched *The Wolf of Wall Street* …
  a [ ] seven times.
  b [ ] four times.
  c [ ] three times.

UNIT 9: Achievement

9a Is it important to go to university?

a Watch video 9a. Match 1–4 with a–d to make sentences.

1 [c] In Mark's opinion
2 [ ] In Carolyn's opinion
3 [ ] In Matt's opinion
4 [ ] In Lauren's opinion

a it isn't necessary to have a degree for some jobs.
b most companies prefer to employ people with degrees.
c it can be very useful to go to university if you want to have a specific career.
d it's important for young people to get the experience of living away from their parents.

9b What advice would you give to a student who doesn't like her university course?

b Watch video 9b and tick (✓) the correct answers.

1 Mark thinks that she should try and change it if ____________ her course.
   a [✓] it's early in
   b [ ] it's late in
   c [ ] it's in the middle of
2 Carolyn thinks that perhaps she should change ____________.
   a [ ] her university
   b [ ] her director of studies
   c [ ] one or two of her modules
3 Matt says that at a lot of universities students can change their ____________ during the first year.
   a [ ] modules
   b [ ] course
   c [ ] tutor
4 Lauren thinks that she should ____________.
   a [ ] talk to her friends
   b [ ] study something different
   c [ ] get a new job

9c What are the advantages of studying online?

c Watch video 9c. Complete the sentences with the names in the box.

~~Mark~~ Matt Lauren Carolyn

1 In ___Mark___'s opinion you don't need to live near the university.
2 In ____________'s opinion you can study when it suits you.
3 In ____________'s opinion it's very good for people that have children.
4 In ____________'s opinion you don't need to go to lectures that start early in the morning.

UNIT 10: Values

10a What would you do if you found a bag of money in the street?

a Watch video 10a and tick (✓) the correct answers.

1 William says that he would ____________.
   a [ ] keep it for himself
   b [ ] take it to the bank
   c [✓] take it to the police station
2 Mitchell says he would ____________ if it was a small amount of money.
   a [ ] take it to the police
   b [ ] keep it for himself
   c [ ] spend it on new clothes
3 Shelby says that she would ____________.
   a [ ] keep it for herself
   b [ ] take it to the police station
   c [ ] give it to her mum
4 Andy says that he would ____________.
   a [ ] spend it on a nice holiday
   b [ ] keep it for himself
   c [ ] take it to the police station

10b How long would you queue in a shop before you gave up and left?

b Watch video 10b and tick (✓) the correct answers.

1 William would queue for …
   a [ ] five minutes.
   b [✓] ten minutes.
   c [ ] fifteen minutes.
2 Mitchell would usually queue for …
   a [ ] ten minutes.
   b [ ] twenty minutes.
   c [ ] thirty minutes.
3 Shelby would queue for …
   a [ ] ten minutes.
   b [ ] twenty minutes.
   c [ ] twenty-five minutes.
4 Andy would queue for …
   a [ ] five minutes.
   b [ ] ten minutes.
   c [ ] twenty minutes.
5 Adam would queue for …
   a [ ] 10–15 minutes.
   b [ ] 15–20 minutes.
   c [ ] 5–10 minutes.

10c Would you complain if you couldn't hear a film in the cinema because other people were too noisy?

c Watch video 10c and underline the correct words to complete the sentences.

1 William *doesn't mind* / *gets annoyed* / *doesn't do anything* if people are talking near him.
2 Mitchell *would complain* / *wouldn't complain* / *would change seats* if someone was talking near him.
3 Shelby would complain *immediately* / *after five minutes* / *after ten minutes* if someone was talking near her.
4 Andy would complain to *the people themselves* / *a cinema employee* / *the manager* if someone was talking near him.
5 Adam would complain to the *people that were making the noise* / *a cinema employee* / *the manager* if someone was talking near him.

UNIT 11: Science & Discovery

11a Would you like to own any kind of robot?

a Watch video 11a. Complete the sentences with the names in the box.

James Dee Dee Petros

1 ____________ would like to have a robot so that it could do the jobs around the house that she doesn't like doing.
2 ____________ would like to have a robot so that he could have more time for working.
3 ____________ would like to have a robot so that he could have more time for sleeping.

11b Have you started using any new technology recently?

b Watch video 11b. Match 1–4 with a–d to make sentences.

1 [c] Petros
2 [ ] Dee Dee
3 [ ] James
4 [ ] Ayden

a doesn't know much about information technology.
b owns a fully electric car.
c has had a smartphone for several years.
d likes to have the latest products.

11c Can you think of three important inventions?

c Watch video 11c and tick (✓) the correct answers.

1 In Petros's opinion, the three most important inventions are …
a [ ] the wheel, the car and computers.
b [ ] the bicycle, the car and the telephone.
c [✓] the wheel, the bicycle and the boat.

2 In Dee Dee's opinion, the three most important inventions are …
a [ ] bicycles, cars and computers.
b [ ] the Internet, computers and cars.
c [ ] electricity, computers and the Internet.

3 In James's opinion, the three most important inventions are …
a [ ] the wheel, the telephone and electricity.
b [ ] the Internet, computers and the telephone.
c [ ] cars, computers and the Internet.

4 In Ayden's opinion, the three most important inventions are …
a [ ] the wheel, the bicycle and cars.
b [ ] cars, boats and computers.
c [ ] the bicycle, microwaves and the Internet.

UNIT 12: Characters

12a When you were a child, did you get on well with your brothers and sisters?

a Watch video 12a. Match 1–5 with a–e to make sentences.

1 [c] Lauren says that
2 [ ] Adam says that
3 [ ] Patrick says that
4 [ ] Oliviero says that
5 [ ] Dana says that

a she got on quite well with her sister when they were little.
b he always got on well with his brother and sister.
c she fought a lot with her brother when they were younger.
d he started getting on well with his older brother when he was about 15.
e he has the same interests as his younger brother.

12b Can you remember something a teacher said to you when you were at school?

b Watch video 12b and tick (✓) the correct answers.

1 Lauren's teacher told her that if you make a mistake …
a [ ] you'll get a bad mark.
b [ ] it's too late to fix it.
c [✓] you can start again.

2 When he was at school, Adam was …
a [ ] hard-working.
b [ ] naughty.
c [ ] lazy.

3 Matteo's teacher said that …
a [ ] he should believe in his own ability.
b [ ] he wasn't very clever.
c [ ] he should work harder.

4 Dana's teacher told her that it's important to …
a [ ] study hard and play hard.
b [ ] follow your dreams.
c [ ] know your place in the world.

12c What kind of things do you normally talk about with your friends?

c Watch video 12c and tick (✓) the correct answers.

1 Lauren and her friends usually talk about …
a [ ] politics and sport.
b [ ] fashion and the weather.
c [✓] the news and fashion.

2 Adam and his friends usually talk about …
a [ ] holidays, sport and fashion.
b [ ] relationships, holidays and work.
c [ ] the news, holidays and the meaning of life.

3 Patrick and his friends usually talk about …
a [ ] cricket and football.
b [ ] tennis and football.
c [ ] basketball and tennis.

4 Matteo and his friends usually talk about …
a [ ] sport, fashion and politics.
b [ ] girls and life experiences.
c [ ] work, the news and sport.

5 Dana and her friends usually talk about …
a [ ] books, school and travel.
b [ ] sport, fashion and politics.
c [ ] work, books and holidays.

AUDIOSCRIPTS

Unit 1

01.01

1 birthday
2 bank
3 cinema
4 food
5 party
6 silly
7 music
8 sport
9 friendly
10 blog

01.02

MEGAN What's Andrea doing in that shop?
NAOMI She's buying some postcards to send to her family.
M Really? I don't usually send postcards. I usually write a message on Facebook. And sometimes I post a few photos of my holiday on Instagram.
N Yes, me too, but Andrea's grandparents don't use social media, so she sends them postcards instead.
M Oh, and what are Marco and Jack doing this morning?
N They're spending the day at the beach.
M But Marco doesn't like swimming in the sea. He says the water's too cold.
N Yes, but it's really hot today!

01.03

Sam Hi, James! Long time no see! How are you?
James Hi, Sam. I'm fine, thanks. What a lovely surprise! Great to see you!
S Yes, it's really nice to see you, too.
J Where are you living these days?
S Oh, not far from here. In Park Road, near the sports centre.
J Oh, how nice!
S And this is my wife, Jackie.
J Your wife – wow! That's fantastic news! Nice to meet you, Jackie.
Jackie Nice to meet you, too.

01.04

1 Sea View Road? Oh, how nice!
2 Your husband – wow! That's fantastic news!
3 We really must go. We're late.
4 What a lovely surprise!
5 Say hello to Roger for me.
6 Long time no see!
7 It was really nice to meet you.
8 We must meet up soon.
9 It was great to see you again.
10 When did we last see each other?

01.05

1 I'm pretty sure it was two months ago.
2 What a lovely surprise!
3 It was really nice to meet you.
4 I'm sorry, but I really must go.
5 Where are you living these days?
6 I'm late for a meeting.

01.06

PRESENTER When you move to a new school or town or start at university, it's important to make new friends. But it isn't easy. On today's programme new students from Durham University tell us how they are making friends during the first few weeks of term. First up is Ollie.
OLLIE I don't particularly like going to parties and I hardly ever go to bars so it was difficult for me to make friends. I like people who I have something in common with, so I joined the university walking club. We meet every Sunday and normally go for a walk into the forests or by the river near the university. It's good fun and I get to meet a lot of different people.
PR Joining a club is a great way to meet new people. But there are other ways. Let's hear from Sophia.
SOPHIA I'm studying drama, so I like talking to people. I'm not particularly interested in joining a club, as I generally prefer to meet people who like a lot of different things. I posted a message on an online student network saying 'I'm looking for some friends. No rude or serious people. We can meet for a drink in the students' café every Tuesday.' About ten people come each week. It's great fun and everyone is different.
PR But if you don't want to start your own group, there are other ways. Over to Ethan.
ETHAN I don't really like using social media to make friends. I'm living in a large student house with about thirty other people so in the first week I knocked on everyone's bedroom door and said hello. Everyone here is friendly. Now I'm rarely on my own and there is often someone to talk to or go out with in the evenings.

Unit 2

02.01

depart	departed	look	looked
love	loved	post	posted
listen	listened	invite	invited
hate	hated	enjoy	enjoyed
sound	sounded	like	liked

02.02

1 Were /wə/ you waiting for the bus?
2 I wasn't driving the car.
3 They were /wə/ watching TV.
4 We weren't having dinner.
5 She was /wəz/ talking on her phone.
6 Was /wəz/ she listening?
7 He wasn't smoking.
8 They weren't playing chess.

02.03

1 Is there anything else I can help you with?
2 Could you tell me where the information desk is?
3 How much is a return ticket to Edinburgh?
4 How often do the buses leave for the airport?
5 What time is the next coach to Barcelona?
6 Can I pay for my ticket in euros?
7 Where can I buy a sandwich for the journey?
8 How much does it cost to get a taxi to the airport?

02.04

A Excuse me.
B Yes, how can I help you?
A Could you tell me which platform the next train to London leaves from?
B Certainly, madam. It leaves from platform 2.
A OK, thanks. And what time does it leave?
B It leaves at 10:32, in twelve minutes.
A Brilliant. Thanks.
B Is there anything else I can help you with?
A Actually, there is one more thing. Where can I buy a cup of coffee? Is there a café near here?
B Yes, there is. There's a café on the platform, over there.
A Great. Thanks so much.
B No problem. Have a good journey.

02.05

1 When did you check into your hotel?
2 How can I help you?
3 Did you get a visa when you went to China?
4 What time did you set off from home?
5 What time is your plane?
6 How much is a return ticket to Bath?

02.06

STEVE And now we go over to Susie with today's traffic and travel news. I hear it is particularly bad on the M3 and M4 motorways?
SUSIE Thanks, Steve, that's right. The heavy rain this morning caused problems on the M3. Four cars hit each other and because of that, there were long delays between London and Guildford. It doesn't look very good on the M4. A lorry broke down near Swindon about three hours ago and there was a huge traffic jam half an hour later. Peter from Bristol just texted on eight seven six six three two to say that there is a queue now. So if you need to get to Swindon this evening, you might want to go off the motorway and go on the main road – the A429.
The M1 is looking a lot better today. There were no delays when I last checked, which is great for anyone who is going to the big music festival in Leeds tomorrow.
Unusually, there aren't many problems on the trains today, but if you are going away this weekend, lots of trains aren't working normally, so check before you go.
If you are flying from Gatwick Airport, please phone your airline before you set off. The computer systems at the airport weren't working this morning and many flights were cancelled today. The computers are working now but there are long delays and even longer queues! Jackie and Bob phoned to say their flight to India was delayed by over twelve hours and they had to check into a hotel at the airport for the night. But I'm pleased to say that they've boarded their plane now and are on their way.
ST Well, I hope they've got a visa or they'll have another long queue when they arrive!
SU I hope so, too! It sounds like they're going to have a real adventure. Back to you, Steve.
ST Thanks, Susie. And here's the latest song by …

Unit 3

03.01

A Good morning. Can I help you?
B Er, yes. I'm looking for a present for my mother.
A Are you looking for anything in particular?
B Well, she loves earrings.
A Really? How about these earrings? They're really beautiful. A perfect present …
B Do you have anything cheaper?
A Well, these earrings here are cheaper. They're only £50 with the discount.
B Yes, I suppose she might like them. On second thoughts, maybe I should get something else.
A OK. Er, let me see … what about this necklace?
B Yes, it's lovely. OK, I'll take it.

03.02

1 Can you show us something else?
2 Can you enter your PIN, please?
3 I'm looking for a present for my husband.
4 Do you have any black jeans?
5 Thanks. I'll take it.
6 Actually, I think we should buy her a book.

03.03

DJ And now it's time for today's talking point. What's the nicest thing you have ever done for someone? Have you given something expensive away to someone or just made someone smile? Call, text or email me now. First on is Anita from Newquay in Cornwall.
ANITA Hello, Baz. My neighbour hasn't got a job at the moment and it's her daughter's thirteenth birthday today. I know she couldn't afford to have a party, so I thought I could help.
DJ And what have you done?
A I've borrowed some speakers from my brother and my friend has made a great playlist of dance music. We've turned part of her back garden into a beach with some sand that I got at the local beach. Lots of the neighbours have given some food and we're going to have a beach party this evening.
DJ That must have made your neighbour smile. Thanks for your call, Anita, and have a great night. What a nice woman. Next we have Gary from Liverpool. What's the nicest thing you've done?
GARY Hi, Baz. Last year I was in the city centre when a tourist asked me how to get to the museum. I gave him directions and then we started talking. He was from Greece and he was really friendly. Then it started raining really hard. He didn't have a coat so I lent him

my umbrella. I asked him to bring it to my house when he was leaving Liverpool and then I forgot about it. Four days later he brought it to my house. I certainly didn't expect that. I invited him in and we had a cup of tea together. We got on well and we became friends. When he left, he invited me to visit him in Greece next summer. I've been saving up and I've just booked my flight. I can't wait!

DJ That's a great story, Gary. Enjoy your holiday! Before we go, I've had an email from Mike in Cardiff. He has started a group called 'Give someone a balloon, make someone smile'. Every Sunday he walks around the city centre with his friends, giving people colourful balloons with smiley faces and hopefully making them smile. Good luck with that, Mike – and have fun!

Unit 4

04.01

A So what have you arranged for this evening?

B Well, my parents are arriving at the station on the 6:30 train from Paris.

A So, are you meeting them at the station?

B Yes, we are. We're taking a taxi from our house at 6:00. I booked it this morning.

A Good. So where are they staying?

B At the Hilton Hotel. They've got a double room with a balcony.

A Great. And what about the restaurant?

B I've reserved a table for eight at eight o'clock. Everyone's coming to the restaurant at 7:45 so we can all be there when they arrive.

A Brilliant. Have you told the restaurant that it's your father's birthday?

B Yes, they've made him a special cake with HAPPY 60TH on it. They're bringing it to our table at ten o'clock, together with the coffee.

A And what about tomorrow?

B They aren't flying to Scotland until the afternoon, so there's plenty of time. Their flight's at 3:30.

A Great, so it's all arranged. I have to go now because I'm meeting Sally for a coffee in ten minutes. See you later!

04.02

1 Are you going to go out tonight?
2 What are you going to do for your birthday?
3 He isn't going to have a holiday this year.
4 We're going to try to find a taxi.
5 I'm going to have a shower after breakfast.
6 They aren't going to do their homework.
7 She's going to phone her brother.
8 I'm not going to go to Ibiza this year.

04.03

1 We want to go swimming today.
2 They won't take you to the old castle.
3 I won't go to that restaurant again.
4 You want to wait for the next train.
5 I want to study English again next year.
6 Tom and I won't invite him to our party.

04.04

A Are you doing anything on Wednesday? Would you like to go for a coffee?

B Oh, that sounds nice. I'll just check. No, sorry, I can't do Wednesday. I'm going shopping with my mother.

A Oh, OK, never mind. How about Friday? Is that OK for you?

B Friday … hang on a minute … no, sorry. I'm going to London for the day. This week's really busy for me.

A OK, so you can't do this week. What are you doing next Monday?

B Next Monday? Just a moment, I'll just check. Nothing! I can do next Monday. Perfect!

A Great! So we can meet for a coffee on Monday?

B Yes, Monday's fine. Where shall we go?

A Shall we meet at *The Coffee Place* at 11:00?

B Brilliant! 11 o'clock. See you then.

04.05

1 Would you like me to bring anything?
2 Are you doing anything this Saturday?
3 This week's really busy for us.
4 What time shall we come round?
5 What are you doing on Tuesday next week?
6 Would you like to come round for lunch?
7 I can't do Thursday this week.
8 Is this Sunday OK for you?

04.06

1 I can't meet you tomorrow.
2 He can meet us at the station.
3 I didn't understand him.
4 She hasn't seen that film.
5 I must start cooking dinner.
6 They don't like basketball.

04.07

ISAAC What are your plans when you finish university this summer, Giles?

GILES Well, my brother Alex is getting married in July.

I That's great news. Where's the wedding?

G His fiancée Laura is Italian so it's going to be in her home town in Tuscany. The town is really pretty.

I That sounds wonderful. Is it going to be a big wedding?

G The party is in the town hall, which is huge. Laura's got a really big family.

I Have you got to do anything at the wedding?

G Yes, I have! I'm going to read a poem I wrote.

I Brilliant! That's exciting. I guess you're going to need a new suit for that.

G Yes, I've got to look my best, especially in front of all those Italian guests.

I Really?

G Yes, they always have great outfits. My dad's going to buy me a new suit if I pass my exams. Something really nice.

I Great! Can you speak any Italian?

G Si. Un po'! But I'm starting lessons next week. The Italian boy in our class, Gavino, is teaching me.

I That's a good idea. How long are you going to Italy for?

G I'm going for two weeks. I'm flying to Rome with my parents on the fourteenth of July and we're going to go sightseeing for a few days. My mum wants to see all the ancient buildings.

I I love Rome. You can walk down a street of really cool modern buildings, then turn a corner and see something that's two thousand years old. It's amazing.

G Wow, I can't wait to go.

I Anyway, I've got to go. I'm going on a date tonight and I want to go to the hairdresser's before it closes.

G OK, well make sure you have a shave before you meet her, Isaac.

I Don't worry, I will. See you tomorrow then.

G OK, see you.

Unit 5

05.01

1 Shall I lend you some money for the bus?
2 Maybe you should ask your manager for the day off.
3 I'll look up the train times online.
4 Do you want me to call a taxi for our guest?
5 Why don't I drive you to the airport?
6 How about arranging a meeting in Mexico City?
7 Why don't you borrow some money from your dad?
8 You could catch a direct flight to Rome.

05.02

1 **A** Shall I book a room for your meeting?
B Yes, good idea.
2 **A** Would you like me to drive you to the station?
B No, I'll be fine. Don't worry about it. I can walk.
3 **A** But you won't be able to have any lunch.
B Oh, never mind. I'm not really hungry.
4 **A** I'm really sorry. I can't go to the cinema tonight.
B Oh, it doesn't matter. We can go another time.
5 How about asking your boss if you can have more time for the report?
6 Why don't I book the train tickets online?
7 Maybe you should invite your boss to the meeting, too?
8 You could send her some flowers for her birthday.

05.03

1 Would you like a coffee?
2 Yes, I would. Thanks.
3 Could you help me with my report?
4 Yes, of course I could.
5 You should get a taxi.
6 Yes, you're right. I should.
7 Shall I book a meeting room?
8 Well, what do you think? Shall I?

05.04

INTERVIEWER Thank you for coming, Josh. First of all, I'd like to talk about your CV. You have some good qualifications, but you've had a lot of different jobs in the last five years. Can you talk about those?

JOSH Yes, I worked as a builder when I finished university. I enjoyed being outside and getting exercise, but I had to work a lot of hours every day and start early in the morning, which I hated, so I decided to look for other jobs.

I So, you don't like working long hours then. Hmm. Tell me about your next job. You worked as a hairdresser, didn't you?

J Yes, I did. I learned a lot of skills while I was there and I really liked the place. But I didn't like having to talk to people every day. I had to talk to the customers and make coffee.

I Hmm. OK. What about your last job? You were an IT worker.

J Yes, that was great. I earned a good salary and I worked with a nice team of people. Sometimes when we were busy I had to work at weekends, which wasn't great, but I usually just worked Monday to Friday. I didn't have to work with people so much, and I could often just sit at my desk and use the Internet, when we weren't busy, of course. And my manager didn't mind what time I started work.

I And what time did you usually start work?

J The latest I could start was 10:30 am.

I OK, Josh, so why would you like to work as a bank clerk for Mainland Bank?

J I'd like to work in a team and get some good experience of working in a bank. It looks like a nice environment to work in. And it also pays really well, too.

I But you don't like working hard or dealing with people every day. Those are important parts of the job.

J Well …

I I'm sorry, Josh, but I don't think you have what we're looking for. Thanks for coming in today and good luck.

J Oh. OK. I thought this would be a good job for me.

I I don't think so. But good luck with your search. Goodbye.

J Bye.

Unit 6

06.01

1 We took my grandmother to the theatre.
2 The children wanted to go to the zoo.
3 Where did you lose your mobile phone?
4 Would you like a cup of coffee?
5 Who did you invite to the party?
6 I don't think you should go to work today.
7 Could I borrow £5, please?
8 What did you think of the food?

06.02

1 **A** I think it's a good idea to book a table. The restaurant might be full.
B Yes, I suppose so. Saturday night can be very busy.
2 **A** Someone stole my handbag when I was at the beach this afternoon.
B How awful! I'm really sorry to hear that.
3 **A** I'd speak to your boss about it.
B I don't think I should do that. She'll be angry with me.
4 **A** I wouldn't worry too much. You can get a new passport at the embassy.
B Yes, you're right. I can go there one day next week.
5 **A** Do you think I should invite Steve to the surprise party?
B No, I don't think that's a very good idea. Anna doesn't like him very much.
6 **A** What do you think I should do?
B I think you should go to the police station.
7 **A** I didn't get the job in marketing.
B Oh, what a pity. I'm sure you'll get another job soon.
8 **A** I broke my finger on Saturday.
B Oh, that's a shame. So that means you can't play tennis today?

06.03

1 Which job do you think I should apply for?
2 I think you should ask your colleagues.
3 I'm really sorry to hear that.
4 Do you think I should look for a new job?
5 I think it's a good idea to speak to your boss.
6 I'd talk to your parents about it.
7 I wouldn't apply for the new marketing job.
8 I don't think you should leave your job.

06.04

1 You're from Canada, right?
2 Elena works in the Spanish Embassy.
3 Would you like to work in London?
4 We're having a surprise party for Anna.
5 My boss wants to speak to me.

06.05

MAYA Hi, Ellie. How are you?
ELLIE Hi. Not so good. I'm getting really annoyed with my little brother Jamie at the moment. I'm trying to revise for my exams and he keeps interrupting me. Sometimes he listens to his music very loud late at night, sometimes he borrows something from me that I need to study, like my dictionary or laptop. I can't concentrate on my work for more than a few minutes. It's terrible.
M You should go and study in the library. It's really quiet there and you won't have to deal with the interruptions. I go there most weekends to study.
OWEN You shouldn't have to go somewhere else. Ask your parents to deal with your brother. Your exams are more important than your brother. Your parents understand that.
E That's a good idea, Owen. I'll ask my dad for help tonight. My brother will listen to him. And I'll also think about going to the library at the weekend. It's nice to have a change sometimes when you're studying. How's your revision going, Owen?
O My problem is I just can't remember anything from history. I read a page and then ten minutes later I've forgotten it.
M That's not unusual. You should try writing down what you've just read. It's amazing how much more you will remember that way.
E And you should also record yourself speaking your notes and then you can listen to them on your phone. You'll be surprised how much you can remember.
O Yes, I'll definitely try those ideas.
E Sometimes I even sing my notes. It's a bit embarrassing, but it will help you to remember lots of information.
O That's a brilliant idea.
M Any advice to help me understand physics? It's so confusing. I look at it, I can read it, I can remember it, but when I think about it, I just don't understand it.
E It doesn't sound like physics is your subject, Maya. Perhaps you should do something else!
O That's not very nice, Ellie. I'm really interested in physics. I'm happy to help you with it if you like, Maya. I think you just need someone to explain it to you.
M Thanks, Owen. I think that Ellie might be right, but I really want to pass the physics exam this year, so I don't have to do it again next year. Are you free this weekend?
O No, I'm afraid not. I need to record all my history notes on to my phone!

Unit 7

07.01

1 **A** So, what's the problem?
B I've got a stomach ache. It's very painful.
2 **A** When did this start?
B About two days ago.
3 **A** Where does it hurt? Can you show me?
B Here, in this area.
4 **A** Can I have a look? So, does it hurt here?
B Yes, it does. It hurts all the time. I can't get to sleep.
5 **A** Are you taking anything for the pain?
B Yes, I've taken some paracetamol.
6 **A** Well, I don't think it's anything to worry about.
B Phew! That's good to hear.
7 **A** I think it's just indigestion.
B Just indigestion? What a relief!
8 **A** I'll give you a prescription for some medicine. Take two pills every four hours.
B OK. Thank you, Doctor.

07.02

1 Don't worry. It's nothing to worry about.
2 Phew! That's good to hear.
3 It hurts all the time. I can't get to sleep.
4 Can I have a look?
5 Are you taking anything for the pain?
6 I feel sick and exhausted.
7 I think you'll need to see another doctor.
8 So, what's the problem?
9 What a relief!
10 You shouldn't stay in bed.

07.03

1 Do you do any exercise?
2 When did this problem start?
3 Could you take a few tests tomorrow?
4 How many pills have you taken?
5 How long have you had this problem?
6 Are you taking anything for the pain?
7 Do you have any allergies?
8 Have you had any accidents recently?

07.04

ORGANISER Welcome to the Lindfield School Reunion – a chance for students who finished school 20 years ago to meet again. It's great to see so many of our old classmates here and I hope that you will all have a brilliant evening. Drinks and dinner will be …
SEAN I haven't seen some of these people for at least 20 years. It's funny to see how everyone has changed.
SARAH I know. I was just talking to Steven Downes. Do you remember him? He used to be really friendly. He was the most popular boy in our class.
SE Yes, I remember Steven. Is that him over there?
SA Yes. He looks serious, doesn't he? Apparently, he just got divorced from Jenny Robertson. She wanted him to get fit and give up smoking and drinking coffee. But you know Steven, he never liked doing what he was told.
SE Yes, I remember! So he hasn't changed that much then. Who's that woman he's talking to? Isn't it Lisa Baker?
SA Yes, I was talking to her earlier. She used to hate doing sport, didn't she? She was telling me that she started getting fit about ten years ago. She's a lot more confident now and a lot healthier. She's going to open her own gym next month.
SE I'm really pleased to hear that. I used to get on well with Lisa.
SA Have you seen Mike Andrews yet? You know, little Mike. He used to be really quiet and he never talked to anyone.
SE Yes, of course.
SA He arrived in a brand-new sports car. He started a computer company and got very rich. That's him talking to Laura Docherty, Emma Alexander and Rachel Edwards.
SE Wow! He looks smart. And he seems to be a lot more popular than he used to be!
SA Ha, yes. Oh wow, look who's just arrived! It's Dale George. With Nicola Walker.
SE Yes, I saw they'd got together on Facebook. It's funny. They used to hate each other.
SA I know. They used to fight and argue all the time. They look really happy now.
SE Yeah. Oh, and what about Martin Dowd? Is he coming? I remember you used to really like him.
SA Yes, he was very popular. I got in touch with him last month to see if he was going to come. Unfortunately, he couldn't. He's getting married this weekend.
SE Again? Is that his third marriage?
SA Yes, that's right. Well, he used to have lots of girlfriends at school. I think he went out with five of the girls in our class.
SE Well, some people never change.
SA Yes, that's true.
O And now, ladies and gentlemen, please take your seats for dinner.

Unit 8

08.01

play squash	go surfing	do gymnastics
play golf	go snowboarding	do yoga
play volleyball	go ice skating	do athletics
play tennis	go jogging	do judo
play football	go rock climbing	do aerobics
play ice hockey	go skateboarding	do karate
play rugby	go scuba diving	
	go windsurfing	

08.02

1 snowboarding
2 athletics
3 jogging
4 gymnastics
5 ice hockey

08.03

1 I meant to send you an email, …
2 I'm sorry I didn't come to your party.
3 I couldn't call you last night …
4 I had to stay late at work yesterday.
5 Sorry, I didn't mean to make you worry.
6 I was going to call you, …
7 I'm sorry I didn't reply to your message, …
8 I had to visit my grandmother yesterday.

08.04

1 I meant to send you an email, but my computer wasn't working.
2 I'm sorry I didn't come to your party.
3 I couldn't call you last night because my phone was dead.
4 I had to stay late at work yesterday.
5 Sorry, I didn't mean to make you worry.
6 I was going to call you, but I couldn't find your number.
7 I'm sorry I didn't reply to your message, but I've been so busy for the last two days.
8 I had to visit my grandmother yesterday.

08.05

MATT Now on Riverside Radio it's time for our weekly guide to what's on this weekend. As usual, we're going to talk to four listeners with very different interests about what they recommend doing this weekend. First of all, we'll talk to Rachel from Albany.
RACHEL Hi, Matt. There's lots happening this weekend if you like outdoor sports. Rock climbing at the Stirling Ranges has started again for the year. All of the climbing routes have been included in the new guidebook, which can only be bought at the information centre. But be careful! This is only for experienced climbers. But if water is more your thing, then the Margaret River Surfers will be out on the water somewhere in the area. Where they meet depends on the waves, but all the information you need is written on their website.
M Thanks, Rachel. That sounds like a lot of fun. Let's talk to Gareth now in Perth.
GARETH Hi, Matt. If you're interested in Italy and art, there's the Italian film festival. It includes films which have been directed by many of Italy's greatest directors and if you go to the art gallery, you can also see photographs of the actors in these films taken by the directors. The films will be shown at the Luna Palace Cinemas.
M Thanks a lot, Gareth. Let's talk to Virginia now in Fremantle. What's your weekend looking like?
VIRGINIA It's all about the written word in Fremantle this weekend. The annual poetry festival, which has been going for ten years, returns. As usual, the festival has been organised by the Fremantle Young Poets Society and includes something for everyone. The highlight this year must be the performance of 'bush poetry' by a group of young poets to music performed by local folk musicians *The Western Arc* on the beach at Wilson Park, south of Fremantle.
M A beach I've been to many times and a lovely place to hear some beautiful music and poetry. Finally, let's talk to Jenny in Bunbury. What's happening in Bunbury this weekend?

JENNY Well, it's time to get active in Bunbury this weekend. It's the annual 10 km race on Sunday. I've been training for the last three months for this, so I'm really looking forward to it. But if you haven't done any training, you're still welcome. Over 1,000 people will be running, jogging, or walking, and I'm sure everyone will enjoy the race, which was won last year by local athlete Jack Harding. It starts at 10 am.

M Well, good luck with it, Jenny. I hope you have a great time. I might come along to support you. So, it sounds like there are lots of things to do this weekend, for people who want to get active, and for those who prefer to get their brains working. I hope you've heard something that you're interested in doing and, most of all, I hope you have a great weekend.

Unit 9

09.01

1 I enjoy studying maths at university, but I hate taking exams.
2 If you take notes in the lesson, it will be easier to revise for the exam.
3 I'm going to work harder next year so that I get better grades.
4 If she fails her exam, she'll have to take it again in January.
5 Although he got excellent grades, he didn't get a place at Oxford University.

09.02

A Is it possible to speak to Diane Smith, please?
B Certainly, I'll just put you through.
C Hello, Diane Smith's phone.
A Oh, hello. Is Diane there, please?
C No, I'm afraid she isn't available. She's in a meeting. Can I take a message?
A Yes, OK. Can you tell her that I called?
C Yes, of course. Who's calling, please?
A This is Paul Roberts speaking.
C OK. Shall I ask her to call you back?
A Yes, please. I'm here all morning.
C Has she got your number?
A Yes, she has.
C Fine. I'll ask her to call you back.
A Thanks. Bye.

09.03

Pam Oh, hello, is that Tom?
Tom Yes, it is.
P Hi, it's Pam here.
T Oh, hi, Pam.
P Is now a good time to talk?
T Well, I'm a bit busy.
P Sorry, Tom. I didn't catch that.
T Yes, I was just saying that I'm busy. Sorry, but I've got a meeting in five minutes. Can I call you back?
P Sure. Is everything OK?
T Yes, fine, but I've got to go.
P OK. Call me when you're free.
T Speak to you soon. Bye.
P Bye.

09.04

1 The film starts at 8:50.
The film starts at 8:15.
2 We're catching the nine o'clock bus.
We're catching the ten o'clock bus.
3 My new boyfriend's name is James.
My new boyfriend's name is John.
4 The programme is on BBC 1.
The programme is on BBC 2.
5 We're going on holiday on Tuesday.
We're going on holiday on Thursday.
6 I was born in 1990.
I was born in 1991.

09.05

PROFESSOR Good morning, Gavino. Thanks for coming to see me this morning.
GAVINO Good morning, Professor.
P I'd like to talk to you about your work. There seem to be a few problems at the moment.
G Problems, Professor?
P Yes. The last two essays that you wrote for me were very poor. I really don't think that you had read any of the books. And you handed them both in late. I know that you're very busy at the moment, but so is everyone, and all the other students managed to do the essays on time.
G I'm sorry, Professor. I had six essays to write this term.
P I know that you only finished secondary school last year, but when you start a degree in psychology, that's what you expect. If your next essay is late, I will refuse to mark it. OK?
G Yes, I understand.
P You've also avoided coming to my class for the last two weeks. If you don't come to class, you won't learn anything, Gavino. This is so important. Do you dislike listening to my lectures or have you got something better to do?
G No, of course not. I really regret not coming, but I was ill. But one of the other students agreed to lend me his notes.
P OK. Well, I recommend reading them very carefully. And if you don't understand something, come and talk to me. There are exams at the end of this term and if you don't attend every lecture, there is a good chance that you will fail.
G Yes, I know. I've started revising for them already.
P Well, that is good news. I've arranged to meet a group of students every Wednesday afternoon to talk about the exam. I think it would be very useful for you to join us.
G Yes, that sounds really useful. Unfortunately, I play rugby every Wednesday. My rugby is very important to me, Professor.
P And your degree isn't?
G Yes, that is very important too. Of course.
P Only 25 students every year get a place to study Psychology at this university. You are very lucky to be here. If your work doesn't get better, you may lose your place on the course. I want you to think very carefully about what is most important to you.
G I will, Professor.
P Have you got any questions that you want to ask me?
G Yes. There is something. Which books should I read?
P The books on the reading list.
G Which list is that?
P The list that I gave you at the start of the term.
G I don't think I have it.
P So you haven't read any of the books then.
G Er, no, I haven't.

Unit 10

10.01

1 If I had lots of money, I would buy an expensive sports car.
2 Would you marry him if he didn't live so far away?
3 If I were you, I wouldn't go swimming in the sea today.
4 If he asked her to go to Argentina with him, she probably would.
5 I would come and stay with you in New York if the flights weren't so expensive.
6 She wouldn't have to drive to work every day if she lived closer to her office.

10.02

1 decision
2 enjoyment
3 complaint
4 description
5 explanation
6 delivery
7 describe
8 complain

10.03

CUSTOMER Good morning. Could you help me, please?
SALES ASSISTANT Yes, of course. How can I help?
C I'd like to return this speaker, please.
SA Would you like to exchange it for something else?
C No, I'd just like a refund, please.
SA Do you have a receipt?
C No, I'm sorry, I don't. It was a present from my boyfriend, but the sound quality is very bad.
SA Well, I'm terribly sorry, but we don't give refunds without a receipt.
C Could I speak to the manager, please?
SA Yes, of course. I'll go and get him.
MANAGER What seems to be the problem?
C I'd like to make a complaint.

10.04

1 Excuse me, but this isn't what I ordered.
2 I'll ask someone to look at that for you right away.
3 We've been here for over an hour, but we still haven't ordered.
4 These shoes don't fit me because they're a bit small.
5 I've changed my mind and I've decided to keep it.
6 I'd like to exchange it for something else.
7 I'd like to return this watch, please.
8 I'll give you a full refund.
9 Your sales assistant hasn't been very helpful.

10.05

1 Can you check my bill, please?
2 Would you like me to give you a refund?
3 Did you bring your receipt with you?
4 Where did you buy it?
5 Could you wait a moment, please?
6 Can you take our order now, please?
7 Can I exchange these jeans for another pair?
8 Could you call the manager, please?

10.06

ZUZA Haluk, you buy a lot of things online, don't you?
HALUK Yes, I do. I think it's really convenient and usually much cheaper than going to a shop. You can go shopping when you feel like it and there are no queues to deal with. I'd do all my shopping online if I could.
Z And never leave your house! What I don't like is that you have to wait a few days for what you've bought to be delivered. That puts me off.
H That's true, but you don't have to wait too long, usually it arrives in one or two days.
Z What was the last thing you bought online?
H I bought a new coat last week.
Z I would never buy clothes online. You can't try them on.
H I saw a photo of the coat and there was also a good description of it.
Z And were you happy with it when it arrived?
H Not really. It was the wrong size. It was too small for me and the colour was different to the photo. The description wasn't very good either. The website said that it was a leather coat, but I don't think it is.
Z Did you complain?
H Yes, I wrote an email to the company and asked for a refund.
Z And what happened?
H They haven't replied yet.
Z Hmm. Well, if I were you, I'd call them and ask for a refund, and an explanation, too.
H Yes, I'll do that next week. I'm sure it will be fine.
Z I wouldn't carry on using that company though. Have you had any other problems buying things online?
H A few. Occasionally things break in the post. And sometimes the delivery drivers are careless with things. I bought a book a few weeks ago and when it arrived, it was completely wet. I think someone had dropped it in some water. But it's usually fine. I buy lots of books online. It's great, because you can find absolutely everything. There's so much more choice than at the local bookshop.
Z Yes, but I enjoy looking around the bookshop. It's really enjoyable.
H Me too. Sometimes I find the book in the shop and then buy it online! It's often a lot cheaper.
Z Hmm, but if everyone did that, there wouldn't be any more bookshops. That would be awful.
H I don't think that would happen.
Z It's happening at the moment. Lots of shops have closed down in our town because people shop online.
H Well, I'm going to carry on shopping online.
Z And I'm going to carry on going to the shops. It's fun, sociable and who knows, I might meet a handsome man in the poetry section of the bookshop. If you went shopping more, you might meet someone. You certainly won't meet anyone sitting at home at a computer.

Unit 11

11.01

1 mountain climbing
2 computer screen
3 science fiction
4 address book
5 bread knife
6 car park
7 coffee cup
8 bookshelf

11.02

A Good morning. Please take a seat. I'll be with you in a moment … Now, how can I help you?
B Could you help us to find a hotel in London, please?
A Yes, of course. Would you like a hotel in the city centre?
B Yes, if possible.
A OK, how about the Grand Hotel? They've got some rooms available.
B Is it near an underground station?
A Yes, it is. It's about five minutes' walk from Marble Arch station. And it's very close to Hyde Park. It's one of the nicest hotels in London.
B Great. Can you ask if they have a double room for three nights? And can you check the price?
A Yes, sure. I'm afraid hotels in London are really expensive. A lot of people think that London's the most expensive city for tourists in the world.
B Yes, the hotel that we stayed in last year cost over £200 a night!
A Let's see … A double room is £130 a night.
B OK, that's fine. We'll take it.
A Right, I've booked it for you. When you come out of the underground station, go along Edgware Road for about 200 metres and it's on the right, opposite the cinema.
B Brilliant. Thanks very much.

11.03

1 accidentally
2 on purpose
3 by chance
4 unfortunately
5 luckily
6 surprisingly
7 amazingly
8 fortunately
9 as expected

11.04

A Can you tell me where the Kensington Meeting Room is?
B Yes, sure. It's on the first floor. Go through that door over there. Then go down to the end of the corridor. Then go up the stairs to the first floor. At the top of the stairs, turn left and go down another corridor. The Kensington Room is the fourth door on the right.
A Great, thanks.

11.05

1 Go down the stairs to the ground floor.
2 Go through those doors and then down the corridor.
3 So first go down the corridor to the stairs?
4 Could you tell me where the staff restaurant is, please?
5 Then go down the corridor and it's the first office on the right.
6 Go up the stairs to the third floor.
7 So, can I just check?
8 OK, I think I've got that.
9 At the top of the stairs, turn right and go down another corridor.
10 The meeting room is the second door on the left.

11.06

1 bored
2 fur
3 sir
4 short
5 ward
6 earl
7 Paul
8 worm

11.07

REPORTER Police are looking for two men who stole money from a cash machine outside Western Bank in Harris Road, Bakersfield at midnight last night. The men arrived at the bank in a large car and crashed into the cash machine on purpose four times. Margaret Edwards is the woman who saw what happened.
MARGARET I live opposite the bank and was in bed at the back of the apartment. But just before midnight, I got up to go to the bathroom. When I heard a car going very fast, I went into the front living room and looked out the window. I've never seen anything like it. The car drove up to the cash machine at about 50 miles per hour and didn't stop. I thought it was an accident, but amazingly they did it again and again. I called the police immediately.
R What did the men do next?
M They got out of the car, put on some gloves and tried to break the cash machine open with a baseball bat which they got from the back of the car. Fortunately, they couldn't open the machine but then, the driver got back into the car and drove into it again.
R Can you describe the men?
M Yes, I can. Fortunately, there were street lights on, so it was easy to see them. The man who was driving the car was about 20 years old, very tall and with very short hair. The other man was about the same age, was short and had dark hair, a hat and sunglasses.
R Erm … how long did it take them to get the machine open?
M Unfortunately, the second time the machine broke and they could steal some money. Luckily, the police also arrived at this time so the men only managed to take a small amount of money. They quickly jumped back into the car and tried to drive off. But they drove backwards into a road sign and then, unsurprisingly, the car didn't start because it was so damaged. So they got out and ran away down Park Avenue.
R Did the police go after them?
M Yes, the police car followed them, but the men ran into the park and disappeared.
R I hear that you found something nearby.
M Yes, I found a key ring with the name Terry on it and a house key. It was next to the car. I think one of the men dropped it. I gave it to the police when they came back.
R And what about the car?
M The police think that the men stole it from a car park earlier in the day.
R Thank you, Mrs Edwards. Photos of the two men which were taken by security cameras outside the bank will be on the TV programme *Everyday Criminals* on RBC1 tonight at 8. And now, over to Adam with today's sports news.

Unit 12

12.01

brought	spoken
come	run
done	taught
fallen	woken
known	won

12.02

1 **A** I believe yoga is a great way to relax before you go to bed.
B You're absolutely right. I do yoga every night.
2 **A** I think Brazil have the best football team in the world.
B I'm not sure about that. I think that Argentina will beat them in the final.
3 **A** In my opinion, Venice is a more attractive city than Florence.
B Definitely. It's such a beautiful place to visit. I love it!
4 **A** This is a nicer cinema than the one we went to last week.
B I agree. The seats are very comfortable and the screen is wider.
5 **A** Barcelona is the biggest city in Spain.
B I don't think so. I think there are more people in Madrid, actually.
6 **A** I think Leonardo DiCaprio is a better actor than Brad Pitt.
B Definitely. He was brilliant in *Once Upon a Time in Hollywood.*
7 **A** In my opinion, Italian coffee is better than French coffee.
B I'm sorry, but how do you know? You don't drink coffee!
8 **A** I think the weather in the UK in winter is much better than in Germany.
B I'm afraid I don't agree. It rains so much here in January and February. I can't stand it!

12.03

1 **A** I think the Amazon is the longest river in the world.
B I don't think so. Actually, I think the Nile is longer than the Amazon.
2 **A** I think Swiss chocolate is much nicer than British chocolate.
B You're absolutely right. It's possibly the best in the world.
3 **A** Russian is a harder language to learn than Spanish.
B Definitely. In my opinion, Spanish is one of the easiest languages to learn.
4 **A** Everybody should retire when they reach sixty.
B Oh, please. That's much too early! Older people have so much experience which they can pass on to their younger colleagues.
5 **A** Tablets are so much more practical than laptops.
B That's true. They're much lighter and easier to carry.
6 **A** His last film was brilliant!
B You're right. It's the best film he's made so far.

12.04

1 **A** Antonio Banderas is a Mexican actor.
B Er, he's actually a Spanish actor.
2 **A** French food's the best in the world.
B Well, actually, I think Italian food is the best.
3 **A** I like the American English accent.
B Do you? I prefer British English, actually.
4 **A** New York's the best place to live in the USA.
B Actually, I think San Francisco's the best place.
5 **A** I think Chelsea will win the Champions League this year.
B No way! Barcelona will win it this year.
6 **A** Baseball is the most popular sport in the USA.
B I'm sorry, but I think American football is the most popular sport.

12.05

DAISY So, where have you been in India so far, Brad?
BRAD I flew into Delhi and took the train down across to Jaipur. I'm going to Goa next. Have you been there, Lewis?
LEWIS Yeah, Goa's cool. We're going to Kerala. How's your trip been so far, Brad?
B Apart from the mosquitoes and the spiders, pretty good. I had a great time in Delhi. I stayed with this Indian guy, Raj, who I'd met through the website Couchsurfing.org. He was really sociable and took me to some really amazing places.
D Yeah, we've met some great Indian people. Really friendly and generous.
B Yeah, but not everyone. I had a pretty bad time in Jaipur.
D What happened?
B I met these two brothers, Jay and Vikram, in a tea house. Jay was really funny and confident. He knew a lot about California. Viki was older and a bit more sensible. They offered to show me around and they seemed reliable so I agreed. We went sightseeing and they told me about their lives. Viki said that they could take me to see some tigers the next day if I wanted.
L Sounds cool.
B Well, then they started telling me about their business. They sold jewellery. They took me to their factory and showed me around. Then they tried to sell me some. I didn't want to, but in the end I said I would buy a small piece. They said it would be ready the next day and then took me back to my hostel. The next day I felt a bit anxious, but went to their factory to collect the jewellery. They had made my piece and had made 30 other necklaces too. They said that this was what I had asked for the day before. They told me that I would have to pay 100 dollars for the jewellery. I had only taken 10 dollars with me when I left that morning. Jay said that he would take me to a cash machine to get the money. I hadn't taken my credit card with me, but I didn't tell him that. We drove to a bank and we all got out. I didn't know where I was, but I decided to run away. I started running and Jay followed me. But I was faster and after a few minutes I was safe. I waited behind a dustbin in a small street for a while and then went onto the main road and found a taxi. The driver could see how anxious I was and drove me back to the hostel. I told him what had happened and he was quite angry with them. He was really generous and didn't charge me anything. The next day I took the first train out of Jaipur!
L Sounds awful. But hey, that's a pretty cool story you've got.
D Yeah.
B Yeah, I know. I'm sure you've got some stories. And we've got another three hours on this train!
L No worries, mate. So, we were in Varanasi …

ANSWER KEY

Unit 1

1A

1

a 2 serious 3 delicious 4 beautiful 5 silly 6 lovely

b 2 delicious 3 perfect 4 strange 5 all right 6 awful 7 amazing 8 rude

2

a 2 did you meet 3 Did he grow up 4 was the film like 5 did you pay
6 Why did she go 7 did he make 8 was your holiday

b 2 Does he work in a bank?
3 Why did you go to New York last month?
4 What is that new Brazilian restaurant like?
5 Who was that man with your sister?
6 What type of TV programmes do you watch?
7 Which university did you go to?
8 How much did the tickets cost?

1B

1

a 2 I particularly enjoy watching old Hollywood films.
3 She absolutely hates it when people are late for meetings.
4 We usually go to Italian restaurants, but sometimes we go to Turkish ones.
5 We're pretty sure his flight arrives at Terminal 2, but I need to check.
6 I really hope he brings his beautiful sister to the party!

b 2 hardly ever 3 usually 4 fairly 5 absolutely 6 rarely 7 really 8 pretty

2

a long vowel: 3, 4, 5, 7, 8

3

a 2 go 3 'm reading 4 wants 5 are you waiting 6 visit 7 's studying
8 're playing

b 2 's buying 3 don't 4 send 5 write 6 post 7 don't use 8 sends
9 are Marco and Jack doing 10 're spending 11 doesn't like 12 's

1C

1

a 2 What a 3 to see you 4 these days 5 far from 6 how 7 this is
8 news 9 meet 10 too

c 2 news 3 must 4 surprise 5 hello 6 time 7 meet 8 up 9 again
10 last

2

a 2 lovely, surprise 3 really, nice, meet 4 sorry, must, go 5 Where, living
6 late, meeting

1D

1

a c

b True: 2, 5; False: 1, 3, 4, 6

2

a 2 Yesterday we visited the Palace of Versailles near Paris.
3 In the mornings, I usually go to the beach with my Portuguese friends.
4 I hope you're having a great time in Canada with your family.
5 Their English is very good, but we always speak in German.

3

a **Possible answer:**

Hi Paul,

I'm spending two weeks with my brother and his family here in Turkey. I'm having a great time and the weather is sunny every day.

My brother's family live about 30 km from the centre of Istanbul in a small town. It's very hot at the moment, but there is a beach near their house.

Every day I visit a new place with my brother's family. Yesterday we went to the Grand Bazaar in Istanbul's Old City. It's an enormous indoor market and there are over 3,000 shops. I'm sending you a photo of it.

How are you? I hope you're still having fun.

See you soon!

Maria

Reading and listening extension

1

a 2 c 3 a

b 2 b 3 c 4 a 5 b

2

a 2 a 3 b

b 2 a 3 b 4 c 5 a 6 b

Review and extension

1

2 At the moment, she's working at the café by the bus station. / At the moment, she is working at the café by the bus station.
3 Why did you miss the bus?
4 I can't talk to you now because I'm doing my homework.
5 What kind of music do you usually listen to?
6 They're waiting for the coach to London. / They are waiting for the coach to London.

2

2 We really enjoyed the film last night.
3 We had a lovely time at the party last night.
4 I think our history lessons are so boring.
5 I think that man's a bit strange. Look, he's talking to himself.
6 New York's all right, but I prefer living in London, actually.

3

2 h 3 a 4 c 5 g 6 f 7 b 8 d

Unit 2

2A

1

a 2 I slept very badly on the plane, so I felt very tired the next day.
3 Did you take the train from New York to Washington?
4 Correct
5 They spent two nights in a hotel and then they stayed at a friend's house for three days.
6 I didn't enjoy my trip to Scotland because the weather wasn't very good.
7 Correct
8 Correct

b 1 **B** didn't sleep, weren't 2 **A** did you do **B** didn't have, decided
3 **A** did Ben go **B** went 4 **A** Did you bring **B** did, bought
5 **A** Did you see **B** did, met 6 **A** Did you visit **B** didn't have

2

a 2 e 3 a 4 f 5 h 6 b 7 c 8 g

b 2 passport 3 backpack 4 guidebook 5 foreign currency 6 suitcase

3

a hated, sounded, posted, invited

2B

1

a 2 gave 3 left for 4 missed 5 took off 6 landed
7 boarded 8 changed 9 got to

b 1 **B** crash 2 **A** miss **B** got lost 3 **A** long delays **B** strike
4 something wrong 5 queue, broke down 6 **B** turbulence

2

a 2 was snowing 3 Were you flying 4 were you driving 5 were you standing 6 wasn't working

b 2 was driving 3 broke down 4 missed 5 bought 6 were waiting 7 started 8 decided 9 took 10 bought

3

a Sound 1: c, e, f; Sound 2: b, g; Sound 3: d, h

2C

1

a
2 Could you tell me where the information desk is?
3 How much is a return ticket to Edinburgh?
4 How often do the buses leave for the airport?
5 What time is the next coach to Barcelona?
6 Can I pay for my ticket in euros?
7 Where can I buy a sandwich for the journey?
8 How much does it cost to get a taxi to the airport?

c 2 can 3 Could you 4 from 5 what time 6 anything else 7 Actually 8 near here 9 over there 10 Have

e 2 b 3 f 4 d 5 h 6 g 7 e 8 a

2

a 2 a 3 a 4 b 5 a 6 a

2D

1

a 1 d 2 c

b True: 2, 3, 5; False: 1, 4, 6

2

a 2 because 3 but 4 and 5 because 6 When 7 so 8 but

3

a **Possible answer:**
Carlos and I got to New York at 14:30 this afternoon. It was a very long flight from Madrid and we were very tired when we arrived because we couldn't sleep on the plane. When we got off the plane, the first thing we noticed was the cold – minus six degrees! It was freezing! Everything they say about New York is true! The people at the airport weren't very friendly and we couldn't understand them because they spoke so quickly. In the end, we took a bus from JFK Airport to Manhattan. We're staying at the Crowne Plaza Hotel near Central Park. The hotel is full of European tourists and everyone was very friendly and helpful. Carlos is telling me to get ready to go and eat, so I have to finish now – more tomorrow.

Reading and listening extension

1

a 2 a, c 3 a, d

b 2 Carl and Sam 3 Carl and Sam 4 Ashish and Bryony 5 Ashish and Bryony

c 2 sunny 3 lift 4 cost 5 morning

2

a 2 e 3 c 4 d 5 b

b 2 c 3 a 4 c 5 b 6 a

Review and extension

1

2 When we got to the station, the train was just arriving.
3 My wife called me while I was waiting for my plane.
4 A man took my wallet while I was in the queue for my ticket.
5 Last year, we went on holiday to Greece for two weeks.
6 I was driving to the airport when I saw the accident.

2

2 My journey from Berlin to London took 15 hours.
3 Last week, I went to Rome on a business trip.
4 The traffic was terrible because it was rush hour.
5 By the time they checked out of the hotel, it was 2 pm.
6 In the afternoon, they went sightseeing in the old town.

3

2 cut 3 took 4 fell 5 75% 6 drove 7 I'm 8 are

Unit 3

3A

1

a
2 Have you ever been to the carnival in Rio de Janeiro?
3 I bought a new TV and smartphone last week.
4 You have never borrowed money from me.
5 Have they ever done any volunteer work?
6 She has never left a big tip for a waiter.
7 Have you ever given any money to a homeless person?
8 I found several good bargains last month.

b
1 **B** gave
2 **A** Has she ever asked **B** asked
3 **A** Have you ever helped **B** helped
4 **A** 've left / have left **B** did you leave
5 **A** Has he ever bought **B** bought

2

a 2 g 3 a 4 h 5 e 6 c 7 d 8 b

b 2 into 3 bank account 4 afford 5 lend 6 borrow 7 spend 8 loan 9 back

3B

1

a 2 h 3 e 4 b 5 g 6 c 7 f 8 a

b 2 give 3 did 4 gave 5 do 6 made 7 doing 8 given

2

a 2 already 3 already 4 yet 5 already 6 yet 7 yet 8 already

b
2 He's already made a payment of £2,000. / He has already made a payment of £2,000.
3 Have you paid Louise back yet?
4 Eva has already spent the money she borrowed from me. / Eva's already spent the money she borrowed from me.
5 I haven't made any new friends at school yet.
6 Has she saved enough money to buy a new phone yet?
7 I've already bought a present for my wife. / I have already bought a present for my wife.
8 They've already given £1,000 to charity. / They have already given £1,000 to charity.

3C

1

a 8, 1, 6, 9, 10, 3, 2, 5, 4, 7

c 2 for 3 in 4 next 5 On second thoughts 6 enter 7 size 8 something else

d
2 I think I'm a size 14.
3 Do you have the same one in blue?
4 Can you tell me how much it is?
5 That's a bit too expensive.
6 Do you have a cheaper one?

2

a 2 <u>en</u>ter, PIN 3 <u>pre</u>sent, <u>hus</u>band 4 black, jeans 5 Thanks, take 6 <u>Ac</u>tually, book

3D

1

a c

b True: 2, 3; False: 1, 4

2

a 7, 5, 2, 4, 1, 3, 6

3

a **Possible answer:**
Hello everyone,
This email is to say a big 'Thank you!' to everyone who helped us raise money for Save the Children over the past 12 months. We have successfully raised £495!
Most of you came to the Save the Children sports day in September. That was a brilliant event and we all had lots of fun. Many of you also came to our 1990s karaoke evening in October. And, of course, next week there's our popular quiz night with big prizes for the winning team.

Save the Children will use our money to save children's lives and to give them a better future. Last year, Save the Children helped ten million children around the world. A small amount can make a big difference. For example, just £3 can save the lives of eight children with a stomach virus.
Would you like to help us raise more money for Save the Children? Email us and we can tell you about our future events. Thanks again for all your help.

Reading and listening extension

1

a 2 100 3 13 million 4 12 million

b True: 1, 3, 5; False: 2, 4

c 2 wrote 3 cost 4 spend 5 get 6 borrow 7 save 8 bought

2

a 2 Anita 3 Mike 4 Anita 5 Gary

b 2 b 3 a 4 b 5 c 6 a

Review and extension

1

2 Have you ever given money to charity?
3 I went to China on business last year.
4 She's already sold her old car. / She has already sold her old car.
5 I haven't bought a birthday present for my brother yet.
6 I've already spent £200 this weekend. / I have already spent £200 this weekend.

2

2 Can you lend me 50 euros, please?
3 I don't have a credit card, so I always pay with cash.
4 James is saving up for a new computer.
5 Our taxi driver was very friendly, so we gave him a big tip.
6 I bought a new laptop in the sales – it was only £250!
7 Have you ever done any volunteer work?
8 Tony owes me £50, but he hasn't paid it back yet.

3

2 in time 3 under 4 like 5 about 6 over 7 spoken 8 a beginner

Unit 4

4A

1

a 2 tie 3 jumper 4 top 5 earrings 6 tights 7 tracksuit
8 underwear 9 sandals 10 high heels 11 bracelet 12 flat shoes

2

a 2 Are you going to invite your cousin to your wedding?
3 They aren't going to get married this year.
4 What are you going to do after university?
5 We're going to visit my relatives in Spain next year.
6 What are you going to wear to the party?

b 2 are 3 meeting 4 're taking 5 are 6 staying 7 's coming
8 're bringing 9 aren't flying 10 'm meeting

3

a 2 gonna 3 going to 4 going to 5 gonna 6 gonna 7 going to 8 going to

4B

1

a 2 h 3 g 4 b 5 f 6 a 7 d 8 e

b 1 **B** 'll 2 **B** 'll 3 shall 4 won't 5 **A** Shall **B** 'll 6 won't
7 Will 8 **B** Will

2

a Across: 5 indoor 7 high 8 ordinary 10 peaceful
Down: 1 modern 2 narrow 3 magnificent 6 noisy 9 huge

b 2 pretty 3 outdoor 4 quiet 5 modern 6 high

3

a 2 won't 3 won't 4 want to 5 want to 6 won't

4C

1

a 3, 10, 5, 2, 1, 6, 7, 4, 9, 8

c 2 Are you doing anything this Saturday?
3 This week's really busy for us.
4 What time shall we come round?
5 What are you doing on Tuesday next week?
6 Would you like to come round for lunch?
7 I can't do Thursday this week.
8 Is this Sunday OK for you?

e 2 my mum 3 to the cinema 4 work conference 5 in Blackpool
6 Saturday

2

a 2 meet, station 3 didn't, understand 4 hasn't, seen, film
5 must, start, dinner 6 don't, like, basketball

4D

1

a d

b True: 2, 4; False: 1, 3, 5

2

a 2 Thanks for inviting me to your party.
3 It would be great to see you.
4 We're free on Saturday and we'd love to come.
5 We're having a party on Saturday.
6 We haven't seen you for ages!

3

a **Possible answer if she can go:**
Hi Sam,
Lovely to hear from you. Yes, I'm fine, thanks. My new job is great, but I'm working very hard.
Thanks for inviting me to your birthday party. I'm free next Saturday, and I'd love to come. Don't worry. I'll bring a huge salad! I'm looking forward to seeing you.
All the best,
Olivia

Possible answer if she can't go:
Hi Sam,
Lovely to hear from you. Yes, I'm fine, thanks. My new job is great, but I'm working very hard.
Thanks for inviting me to your birthday party on Saturday. I'm really sorry, the party sounds like fun, but I'm afraid I can't come. I'd love to come, but I'm visiting my cousin in Barcelona next weekend.
Hope you have a nice birthday party. See you soon.
Love,
Olivia

Reading and listening extension

1

a 6, 4, 5, 3, 2, 1

b True: 2, 3, 5; False: 1, 4

c 2 going to have, hasn't bought / has not bought
3 is going to / 's going to
4 is getting ready / 's getting ready
5 is arriving / 's arriving

2

a 2 Alex 3 Gavino 4 Giles's mum 5 Isaac

b 2 b 3 b 4 c 5 b

Review and extension

1

2 Don't worry. I will pay the money back tomorrow. / Don't worry. I'll pay the money back tomorrow.
3 He's going to buy a new car next month. / He is going to buy a new car next month.
4 Shall I come to your house in half an hour?
5 Shall we go to that café for a coffee?
6 Are you going to do your homework this evening?

2

2 Are you going to buy a new suitcase in the sales?
3 I love it here in the country. It's so peaceful!
4 He always wears a tie when he goes to a job interview.
5 I love coming to this park because you can't hear the traffic. It's so quiet here.
6 That restaurant's so noisy. It's really hard to talk there.

3

2 for 3 forward 4 well 5 around 6 up

Unit 5

5A

1

a 2 hairdresser 3 plumber 4 scientist 5 banker 6 electrician 7 lawyer 8 accountant 9 chef 10 nurse

b 2 salary 3 training 4 environment 5 team 6 university degree 7 people 8 self-employed 9 skills 10 qualifications

2

a 2 can't 3 can't 4 have to 5 have to 6 can't

b 2 can't 3 don't have to 4 have to 5 doesn't have to 6 has to 7 has to 8 mustn't 9 has to 10 doesn't have to

5B

1

a 2 h 3 a or f 4 g 5 b 6 a or f 7 e 8 d

b 2 might 3 won't 4 might not 5 will / 'll 6 **A** will / 'll **B** will 7 might 8 won't

2

a 2 builder 3 computer programmer 4 vet 5 designer 6 architect 7 musician 8 actor 9 journalist 10 taxi driver 11 shop assistant 12 politician

b 2 builder 3 musician 4 architect 5 shop assistant 6 actor 7 carer 8 computer programmer 9 journalist 10 designer 11 taxi driver 12 politicians

5C

1

a
2 Maybe you should ask your manager for the day off.
3 I'll look up the train times online.
4 Do you want me to call a taxi for our guest?
5 Why don't I drive you to the airport?
6 How about arranging a meeting in Mexico City?
7 Why don't you borrow some money from your dad?
8 You could catch a direct flight to Rome.

c 1 **B** idea 2 **A** Would **B** fine, worry 3 **B** mind 4 **A** sorry **B** matter 5 about 6 don't 7 Maybe 8 could

2

a 2 strong vowel 3 weak vowel 4 strong vowel 5 weak vowel 6 strong vowel 7 weak vowel 8 strong vowel

5D

1

a c

b True: 1, 3, 4, 6; False: 2, 5

2

a 2 f 3 d 4 a 5 h 6 c 7 b 8 e

3

a **Possible answer:**
Dear Sir/Madam,
I am writing to apply for the job of sales assistant, which you advertised on abc-jobs.co.uk.
I am a student at the University of Sussex, and I am available to work starting in October.
A job with you will be an exciting opportunity for me to learn new skills and to work in a new environment. I have a lot of experience working in sales. Last summer, I worked for three months in a very busy shop selling mobile phones and computers, and I think this experience will be very useful in this job.
I attach a copy of my CV with more details about my previous employment.
Could you give me more information about the salary and working hours, and also more details about your training programme?
I look forward to hearing from you.
Yours faithfully,

Reading and listening extension

1

a 1 a 2 c 3 d 4 b

b
2 is doing something they love
3 gets paid well, is doing something they love, (sometimes) has to work long hours every day
4 gets paid well, works and studies, is doing something they love, has to work long hours every day

c 2 b 3 a 4 c 5 a, d

2

a 2 Builder, Hairdresser, Bank clerk 3 Hairdresser 4 IT worker, Bank clerk 5 IT worker, Bank clerk

b
1 early
2 skills, people/customers/clients
3 starting, weekends/the weekend

Review and extension

1

2 Excuse me, sir. You can't eat in the laboratory. It's against the rules. / Excuse me, sir. You mustn't eat in the laboratory. It's against the rules.
3 Do you have to wear a suit to work?
4 When I finish school, I might go to university. It depends on my grades. / When I finish school, I may go to university. It depends on my grades.
5 I have to start work at 7 o'clock in the morning in my new job!
6 I'll take my umbrella. It might rain this afternoon. / I'll take my umbrella. It may rain this afternoon.

2

2 My sister works as a shop assistant in a big department store.
3 You need good qualifications if you want to become a doctor.
4 He works as a designer for a top fashion magazine.
5 If you want to become a plumber, you'll need to do a training programme.
6 My brother wants to become a professional musician.

3

2 job 3 work 4 work 5 work 6 work 7 work 8 jobs 9 work

Unit 6

6A

1

a 2 go 3 Don't sit 4 shouldn't have 5 Eat 6 shouldn't drink 7 don't use 8 should read 9 should have 10 should go

b
2 Eat a lot of fruit and vegetables every day. / You should eat a lot of fruit and vegetables every day.
3 Don't use your computer for very long in the evenings. / You shouldn't use your computer for very long in the evenings.
4 You should try to relax for an hour before you go to bed. / Try to relax for an hour before you go to bed.
5 I think she should get more exercise during the day.
6 You shouldn't go swimming immediately after lunch.
7 When you have a headache, drink some water. / When you have a headache, you should drink some water.
8 Don't stay at work after six o'clock.

2

a 2 h 3 d 4 g 5 f 6 a 7 b 8 c

b 2 on 3 for 4 about 5 for 6 on 7 from 8 for

3

a 2 long 3 long 4 short 5 long 6 short 7 short 8 long

6B

1

a 2 exciting 3 interested 4 shocked 5 annoyed 6 tiring 7 amazing 8 embarrassed

b 2 confused 3 interesting 4 surprising 5 frightened 6 disappointed 7 shocking 8 excited

2

a
2 It was interesting to learn about sharks.
3 Can you tell us where to park our cars?
4 It is dangerous not to wear a seat belt.
5 She had a bath to help her relax.
6 They went to the bus station to meet their aunt.
7 She called her father to ask him for some money.
8 He didn't know what to wear to the party.

b 2 He asked me how to get to the airport.
3 She was annoyed not to receive an invitation to his wedding.
4 They went to the supermarket to buy some food for dinner.
5 We couldn't remember which bus to catch to the airport.
6 John and Angela decided not to have their wedding in Ireland.
7 It was embarrassing to fail my driving test again.
8 She went to the library to borrow a book about dinosaurs for her son.

6C

1

a 2 e 3 f 4 g 5 c 6 h 7 a 8 b

c 2 I think you should ask your colleagues.
3 I'm really sorry to hear that.
4 Do you think I should look for a new job?
5 I think it's a good idea to speak to your boss.
6 I'd talk to your parents about it.
7 I wouldn't apply for the new marketing job.
8 I don't think you should leave your job.

2

a 2 a 3 b 4 b 5 a

6D

1

a c

b True: 3, 5; False: 1, 2, 4

2

a 2 It's a good idea to read something in English every day. For example, you can read different newspapers online.
3 Why don't you do something relaxing this evening, such as going for a swim after work?
4 There are more enjoyable ways of preparing for an exam. For example, you could study with a friend who's in the same class.
5 You could start a new hobby to help you relax, such as dancing or swimming.

3

a **Possible answer:**

Dear Kento,

Thanks for your message. I'm glad that you've written to me asking for some ideas.

I remember when I was learning Japanese, listening was the most difficult thing for me, too. I could understand when my teacher was talking to me, but it was very hard to understand when other people were speaking. Here are some ideas to help you improve your listening in English.

First of all, don't worry if you don't understand every word you hear. That's impossible! You should concentrate only on the most important words. Secondly, try to get extra listening practice outside the classroom. For example, you can go to the study centre and try their listening exercises, such as the audio tracks from your Student's Book. You should also listen to the radio in English and watch British or American TV. It's a good idea to watch films with the subtitles. Next, you can also try listening to podcasts. It's easy to download short stories onto your computer or phone. Finally, it's a good idea to listen to pop songs while you read the words at the same time. There are lots of websites that give you the words of the most popular pop songs.

I hope this helps and please feel free to talk to me after class next week.

Good luck,

Tina

Reading and listening extension

1

a 2 Jade 3 Jade 4 Jade 5 customers 6 Eva

b 2 b 3 a 4 c 5 c

c 2 b 3 a 4 d 5 e

2

a 2 Maya 3 Owen 4 Ellie 5 Owen

b 2 c 3 c 4 b 5 b 6 a

Review and extension

1

2 I think he should do some exercise every day.
3 You should read a book to help you relax.
4 She asked me to drive her to the station.
5 My father taught me how to play the guitar.
6 What should I do if I can't sleep well?

2

2 I was thinking about that TV programme I saw last night.
3 My uncle paid for the tickets and bought popcorn for us as well.
4 I can't afford to spend a lot of money on a holiday this year.
5 My little sister isn't very interested in fashion.
6 I didn't hear the phone because I was listening to some music.
7 I didn't think that horror film was frightening. What about you?
8 I didn't have any money, so I had to borrow £20 from my brother.

3

2 lent 3 brought 4 wrote 5 paid 6 read 7 sold 8 described

Unit 7

7A

1

a 2 hottest 3 colder 4 cold 5 smallest 6 big 7 larger 8 more expensive

b 2 I think it's the most exciting film I've ever seen.
3 My sister is happier than she's ever been.
4 It's hard to understand her because she speaks more quickly than you.
5 He went to one of the best universities in the USA.
6 The weather's much warmer than it was yesterday.
7 She worked harder than her sister and got 95% in her exam.
8 He speaks English much better now than a year ago. / Now he speaks English much better than a year ago. / He speaks much better English now than a year ago.

2

a 2 get in touch with 3 got work 4 got to know 5 got together 6 get ill 7 get paid 8 got divorced

b 2 got married 3 got engaged 4 get a place 5 got rich 6 got an offer 7 got to know 8 got paid

7B

1

a 2 f 3 g 4 b 5 d 6 a 7 h 8 e

b 2 put on, healthy 3 stress 4 get 5 gave up 6 lack of 7 allergies 8 smoker

2

a 2 We didn't use to have 3 we didn't use to go 4 we used to invite 5 he used to cook 6 we used to watch 7 used to play 8 didn't use to complain 9 Did you use to live 10 did you use to live

b 2 didn't use to buy 3 did, use to eat 4 used to speak 5 used to take 6 Did, use to play 7 didn't use to have 8 used to watch

7C

1

a 2 g 3 h 4 e 5 f 6 c 7 a 8 b

c 2 hear 3 hurts, get 4 look 5 taking 6 sick 7 you'll 8 problem 9 relief 10 shouldn't

e 6, 8, 3, 1, 5, 4, 2, 7

2

a 2 down 3 up 4 down 5 down 6 up 7 up 8 up

7D

1

a c

b True: 2, 5; False: 1, 3, 4

2

a 2 After 3 Soon 4 a while 5 Then 6 the end

3

a **Possible answer:**

About two years ago, I used to travel to work every day by bus. It was an awful journey because of all the traffic and sometimes it took me over an hour to get there. So I decided that I needed to find a quicker way to travel to work. I decided to buy a bicycle. The problem was that I wasn't very fit.

I bought an old bicycle from a friend of mine. At first, I was frightened of cycling on the road with all the cars and lorries. To begin with, I took my bike to the little park near my house every day and cycled very slowly for about five or ten minutes. After a while, I started cycling along the quiet roads to the shops about two kilometres from my house. Then I started cycling the five kilometres from my house to the city centre. In the end, I went everywhere on my bicycle!

Now I cycle eight kilometres to work every day and I feel really fit and healthy. It only takes me 30 minutes to get to work, so I save an hour every day.

Reading and listening extension

1

a 2 a 3 d 4 b

b 2 used to be, in the past 3 used to have, in the past
4 used to smoke, in the past 5 are, now

c 2 a 3 c 4 b 5 c

2

a 2 Martin Dowd 3 Steven Downes 4 Dale George 5 Lisa Baker

b 2 smoking, drinking 3 fitness, healthier / fitter
4 gym 5 richer / wealthier 6 like

Review and extension

1

2 I think São Paulo is the biggest city in Brazil.
3 My brother didn't use to like coffee when he was a teenager.
4 This exercise is easier than the last one.
5 I'm studying harder this year than last year.
6 Sydney is the most expensive city in Australia.

2

2 You'll have to do exercise every day if you want to keep in shape.
3 My brother has got a new job and gets paid very well.
4 She loves her boyfriend and I think they'll get engaged soon.
5 While he was at university, he got to know Percem.

3

2 g 3 c 4 b 5 a 6 e 7 d

Unit 8

8A

1

a 2 album 3 classical music 4 architecture 5 novel 6 sculpture
7 photograph 8 painting

b 2 M 3 L 4 A 5 L 6 A

2

a 2 wasn't made / was not made 3 was designed 4 was given
5 were finished 6 were made 7 was designed 8 was found
9 was created 10 were taken 11 was put 12 was finished
13 is visited

b
2 The Eiffel Tower was built in 1889.
3 The novel *Nineteen Eighty-Four* was written in 1948 by George Orwell. / The novel *Nineteen Eighty-Four* was written by George Orwell in 1948.
4 The 2012 Olympic Games were held in London.
5 The film *Schindler's List* was directed by Steven Spielberg in 1993. / The film *Schindler's List* was directed in 1993 by Steven Spielberg.
6 The best coffee is grown in Colombia.
7 Over 17 million new cars were sold in the USA in 2018. / Over 17 million new cars were sold in 2018 in the USA.
8 5,000 bicycles are produced by this factory every year. / 5,000 bicycles are produced every year by this factory. / Every year, 5,000 bicycles are produced by this factory.

8B

1

a
1 **B** 've loved / have loved, since
2 **A** Have you lived, for **B** 've lived / have lived
3 **A** have you been **B** 've been / have been, since, 've known / have known, for
4 **A** have you had **B** 've had / have had, since
5 **A** have you worked **B** 've been / have been, for

b 2 've known 3 's been 4 's had 5 've been, worked 6 's had

2

a play: squash, golf, volleyball, tennis, rugby, football, ice hockey
go: surfing, snowboarding, ice skating, jogging, rock climbing, skateboarding, scuba diving, windsurfing
do: yoga, athletics, aerobics, karate, judo

c Across: 8 windsurfing 10 skating 11 climbing 12 yoga;
Down: 1 hockey 2 snowboarding 3 athletics 4 golf 6 surfing
7 jogging 9 diving

3

a 2 b 3 a 4 b 5 a

8C

1

a
2 I'm sorry, I couldn't come to your party yesterday because I was ill.
3 I couldn't email you because my wi-fi wasn't working.
4 I didn't mean to be late for the meeting, but the train was delayed.
5 I'm really sorry I didn't buy you a present, but the shops were closed.
6 I'm sorry I didn't call you last night, but my phone wasn't working.
7 I was going to finish the report by today, but I've been so busy.
8 I meant to send you a birthday card, but I couldn't find your address.

b 2 couldn't 3 mean 4 matter, fine 5 going to 6 meant
7 worry, fault 8 had to

2

a 2 down 3 up 4 down 5 down 6 up 7 up 8 down

b More to say: 1, 3, 6, 7

8D

1

a c

b True: 1, 4, 5; False: 2, 3

2

a 2 However 3 although 4 However 5 Although 6 although

3

a **Possible answer:**
War Horse by Michael Morpurgo is the story of Joey, a horse that is sold to the British Army at the beginning of the First World War. He is sent to France and is ridden by Captain Nicholls. However, Captain Nicholls is killed in the fighting and Joey is given to a younger soldier named Warren. While he is with Warren, Joey becomes friends with another horse named Topthorn, and they have lots of adventures during the war. Later in the story, Joey and Topthorn are taken by the Germans. Topthorn is killed, but Joey works for the German army until the end of the war.
Although this book was written for children, I really enjoyed it. The story is really interesting and the characters are described very well. You can really imagine what the First World War was like. It's a beautiful story, although it's also very sad and it made me cry. However, there is a happy ending because at the end of the war, Joey is returned to Albert, who was his original owner before he was sold to the army. I couldn't put the book down until I got to the end, and I would definitely recommend it.

Reading and listening extension

1

a True: 1, 2, 5; False: 3, 4

b 2 Sam Lee 3 *To Sleep To Dream* 4 *Flathampton* 5 *To Sleep To Dream, Flathampton*

c 2 a 3 c 4 b 5 a

2

a 2 Stirling Ranges 3 Margaret River 4 Bunbury 5 near Fremantle
6 Stirling Ranges, Bunbury, Margaret River

b 2 The sea 3 film directors 4 listen to 5 Jenny

Review and extension

1

2 I have known Veronica since I was a child. / I've known Veronica since I was a child.
3 We've lived in Edirne for more than ten years.
4 The Sydney Opera House was designed by Jørn Utzon.
5 I taught at that university from 2016 to 2019.
6 I have played golf since I was 12 years old.

2

2 Skateboarding is a great way for children to get fit.
3 Have you got a photograph of your girlfriend?
4 Let's play golf this afternoon.

5 These days, ice skating is popular in New York City during the winter.
6 When I was at school, I had to do gymnastics every Wednesday.
7 The *Mona Lisa* is one of the most famous paintings in the world.
8 Let's go surfing this afternoon.

3

2 the way 3 mistake 4 bus 5 heart 6 hand 7 far 8 next Monday

Unit 9

9A

1

a Across: 3 drama 4 law 5 engineering 7 art
Down: 1 psychology 2 management 6 education

b 2 degree 3 essays 4 fail 5 revise 6 handed 7 notes 8 place
9 get 10 pass

2

a 2 I'll go to Canada on holiday if I can find a cheap flight.
3 If they revise every day, they might pass their exams.
4 If she does well in her exams, she might get a place at Cambridge University.
5 She'll have to get excellent marks if she wants to study medicine at university.
6 I'll call him tomorrow morning if he doesn't reply to my email tonight.
7 Your teacher might give you a bad mark if you don't hand in your essay on time.
8 If you fail your exams, you won't get into university.

3

a 2 If you take notes in the lesson, // it will be easier to revise for the exam.
3 I'm going to work harder next year // so that I get better grades.
4 If she fails her exam, // she'll have to take it again in January.
5 Although he got excellent grades, // he didn't get a place at Oxford University.

9B

1

a 2 not to take 3 trying 4 to see 5 not to fail 6 not taking 7 to speak
8 to go 9 spending 10 not doing

b 2 to take 3 going 4 to get 5 playing / to play 6 to meet 7 reading
8 snowing / to snow

2

a 2 recommended 3 disliked 4 forgot 5 agreed 6 imagined 7 missed
8 avoid 9 managed 10 regretted 11 seemed 12 refused

b 2 avoids 3 arrange 4 forgot 5 recommends 6 miss 7 refuse
8 disliked 9 seems 10 manage

9C

1

a 9, 7, 3, 2, 5, 4, 8, 1, 6, 10

c 2 it is 3 it's 4 good time 5 catch that 6 just saying 7 I've got
8 call you back 9 got to go 10 Call 11 soon

2

a 2 a 3 a 4 b 5 a 6 b

9D

1

a c

b True: 1, 3; False: 2, 4, 5

2

a 2 They 3 She's 4 her 5 one 6 He, he 7 us 8 It, it

3

a **Possible answer:**
Tell us about you …
Hello, everyone. I'm Hitomi and I come from Osaka, in Japan. I'm doing a Master's degree in economics at Tokyo University and next year I want to get a job in London or New York. I studied English for ten years at school, so I can write it quite well, but I can't speak it very well, so I need to practise!
How do you feel about this online course?
I really want to learn more about American films because I've always loved watching them. I hope the course will help me improve my English. I'm looking forward to talking about all the films we're going to watch with the other students on the course. I'm sure my English will improve quickly during the course.
What do you do when you're not studying?
When I'm not studying, I play a lot of sport. I play tennis once or twice a week and sometimes golf at the weekend. I also go to the gym at the university because I like keeping really fit. Sometimes I do yoga when I feel stressed. It really helps me relax.

Reading and listening extension

1

a 2 medicine 3 law 4 psychology

b 2 c 3 a 4 b 5 b

c 2 the UK 3 speaks 4 studying 5 work / a job

2

a True: 1, 2, 6; False: 3, 4, 5

b 2 f 3 e 4 a 5 c 6 d

Review and extension

1

2 I want you to buy me some bread and milk from the shop.
3 We won't play golf this afternoon if it rains.
4 She enjoys reading books about dinosaurs.
5 Will you go to university next year if you get good grades?
6 I've just finished having dinner with my family.

2

2 He did really well at school and got into a good university.
3 She got a very bad grade on her last history essay.
4 Although they worked hard, they both failed their maths exams.
5 She always took taxis because she disliked waiting for buses.
6 He did a degree in medicine and now he's a doctor.

3

2 away 3 down 4 off 5 on

Unit 10

10A

1

a 2 Would you complain if the waiter made a mistake with your bill?
3 What would you do if there were no teachers at school?
4 If I cycled to work, I could save a lot of money on petrol.
5 I would feel less stressed if I did yoga every day.
6 If I missed the last bus, I'd have to take a taxi.
7 I could stop working if I became rich.
8 If you found the film on the Internet, would you download it?

b 2 Could you work, needed
3 was, I'd complain
4 I could take, wasn't
5 walked, you'd feel
6 stopped, 'd take
7 wouldn't walk, were
8 would you do, lost

2

a 2 g 3 d 4 c 5 f 6 e 7 b 8 a

b 2 off 3 round 4 like 5 up 6 in 7 after 8 on

3

a 2 unstressed 3 stressed 4 stressed 5 unstressed 6 stressed

10B

1

a 2 a little 3 no 4 much 5 much 6 many 7 many 8 any 9 a few
10 any 11 some

b 2 too much 3 enough milk 4 too 5 clearly enough 6 too many
7 too quickly 8 big enough

2

a Across: 6 decision 8 delivered 9 complaint 10 complain
Down: 1 choose 2 decided 4 description 5 enjoy 7 explain

3

a 2 b 3 b 4 a 5 b 6 a 7 b 8 b

10C

1

a 7, 1, 4, 2, 6, 5, 8, 3

c 2 I'll ask someone to look at that for you right away.
3 We've been here for over an hour, but we still haven't ordered.
4 These shoes don't fit me because they're a bit small.
5 I've changed my mind and I've decided to keep it.
6 I'd like to exchange it for something else.
7 I'd like to return this watch, please.
8 I'll give you a full refund.
9 Your sales assistant hasn't been very helpful.

2

a 2 b 3 a 4 b 5 b 6 a 7 b 8 a

10D

1

a 1 Email C 2 Email A 3 Email B

b True: 1, 4; False: 2, 3, 5

2

a 2 Thank you very much for your email of 15 June.
3 I am writing to apologise for the poor service you received in our restaurant last Saturday.
4 We have just opened the restaurant, and we have had a few problems finding experienced waiters.
5 However, we are working hard to improve our levels of service and I am confident that we will not have any more problems like this in the future.
6 We hope you will come back to our restaurant again and we would like to offer you a 50% discount on your next meal with us.
7 This is our way of apologising for the problems you have had.
8 Yours sincerely,

3

a **Possible answer:**

Dear Mr Hurst,

Thank you for your email of 10 July about the problems you had during your stay at our hotel. I am writing to apologise for the poor service you had while you were staying with us.

Unfortunately, we have had a few problems with our website recently. I think that is why you were not given a room with a sea view. We have also had some problems with our water heating system in the last few weeks, so this is why sometimes there was not enough hot water for showers or baths. Finally, we did not have enough staff in our restaurant while you were staying with us because three of our waiters became ill.

I hope you will come and stay at our hotel in Nerja again. I would like to offer you a 50% discount the next time you come to the Hotel Dante. This is our way of apologising for the problems you have had.

Yours sincerely,

Fabián García

Manager

Hotel Dante

Reading and listening extension

1

a 2 c 3 a

b 2 a 3 b 4 a 5 b

c 2 b 3 b 4 c 5 a 6 a, b 7 c 8 c

2

a 2 Zuza 3 Zuza 4 No one 5 Haluk 6 Zuza

b 2 c 3 c 4 b 5 b 6 c

Review and extension

1

2 He invited too many people to his party – over 100!
3 If I had a motorbike, I wouldn't take the bus to work.
4 This morning it was too cold to swim in the sea.
5 I would go on a diet if I were overweight. / I'd go on a diet if I were overweight.
6 If Chile won the World Cup, he would be delighted.

2

2 Tim isn't here at the moment, but I can pass on a message.
3 The restaurant only has a small menu, so the choice of food is very limited.
4 It's sad that Ana and Esteban have broken up after being together for ten years.
5 If you aren't happy with your hotel, you should make a complaint. / If you aren't happy with your hotel, you should complain.
6 She was offered a better job, but she turned it down.

3

2 go 3 put 4 keeps 5 put 6 carry 7 got 8 kept

Unit 11

11A

1

a 2 where 3 which 4 who 5 where 6 who 7 which 8 which 9 where 10 who

b 2 There's a woman over there that used to work for your company. / There's a woman over there who used to work for your company.
3 There's a café near me which has 50 different kinds of tea! / There's a café near me that has 50 different kinds of tea!
4 My dad has a cousin in Houston who works for NASA. / My dad has a cousin in Houston that works for NASA.
5 I know an Italian restaurant in London where you can have chocolate spaghetti!
6 I got a new phone which also comes with free music apps. / I got a new phone that also comes with free music apps.
7 That's the cinema where they're showing the new Superman film next week.
8 He's just bought a new TV which has amazing picture quality. / He's just bought a new TV that has amazing picture quality.

2

a Across: 4 science fiction 5 bread 8 road sign 11 rock star
Down: 1 ring 2 coffee 4 soundtrack 6 address 7 lights 9 screen 10 cars

3

a 2 com<u>pu</u>ter screen 3 science <u>fic</u>tion 4 <u>add</u>ress book 5 <u>bread</u> knife 6 <u>car</u> park 7 <u>co</u>ffee cup 8 <u>book</u>shelf

11B

1

a 2 a 3 a 4 Ø 5 a 6 the 7 an 8 Ø 9 Ø 10 the 11 a 12 the 13 Ø 14 Ø 15 the 16 Ø 17 the 18 the 19 the 20 Ø 21 the 22 the

c 2 In the UK, police officers don't usually carry guns.
3 I love Italian ice cream. It's the best in the world!
4 They drove to Paris by car and stayed in a lovely hotel near the Eiffel Tower.
5 France is the most popular country for tourists in the world.
6 Doctors in the USA are paid much more than nurses.

2

a 2 g 3 a 4 d 5 b 6 e 7 h 8 c

b 2 Unfortunately 3 by chance 4 Luckily 5 on purpose 6 Amazingly

3

a 2 a 3 b 4 b 5 a 6 b 7 a 8 a 9 b

11C

1

a 4, 6, 1, 3, 5, 2

c 2 Go through those doors and then down the corridor.
3 So, first go down the corridor to the stairs.
4 Could you tell me where the staff restaurant is, please?
5 Then go down the corridor, and it's the first office on the right.
6 Go up the stairs to the third floor.
7 So, can I just check?
8 OK, I think I've got that.
9 At the top of the stairs, turn right and go down another corridor.
10 The meeting room is the second door on the left.

2

a 2 fur 3 sir 4 short 5 ward 6 earl 7 Paul 8 worm

11D

1

a b

b True: 1, 3, 5; False: 2, 4

2

a 2 as 3 because 4 because of 5 As 6 as a result of
7 Because of 8 because

3

a **Possible answer:**
In my opinion, the most important invention of the last 25 years has been the mobile phone. Before it was invented, if you wanted to speak to somebody on the phone, you had to be at home, in the office or in a public phone box. With a mobile phone, it is much easier to keep in contact with your friends, your family and your colleagues than before. You can have a conversation wherever you are – on the street, at the supermarket, in a car or on a train. Because of this, it is also easier for people to stay in touch with their children or with their elderly relatives. It is also very useful to have a mobile phone if you have an accident or if you need to call the police. These days, mobile phones are not only devices that let you make phone calls and send texts. You can also take photos, record videos, listen to music, check the Internet and talk to your friends on social media. I believe it's the most useful thing I have. In fact, I don't know where I would be without mine.

Reading and listening extension

1

a 2 plane / aeroplane 3 rainforest / forest 4 sweets 5 river 6 boat 7 hospital

b True: 1, 2; False: 3, 4, 5

c 2 b 3 e 4 c 5 a 6 f

2

a 5, 3, 6, 7, 4, 2, 1

b 2 a 3 c 4 a 5 b 6 b

Review and extension

1

2 Sorry, I can't talk to you at the moment because I'm at work.
3 Generally speaking, most men like watching sport on TV.
4 Modern Living is the shop where I bought my leather sofa.
5 Look! That's the man who stole my wallet!
6 John F Kennedy was the American president who was assassinated in Dallas in 1963. / John F Kennedy was the American president that was assassinated in Dallas in 1963.

2

2 I think I wrote his phone number in my address book.
3 Surprisingly, it tasted a bit like chicken.
4 I'm afraid of heights, so I don't want to go rock climbing.
5 He opened the car door without looking and hit an old man on a bicycle.
6 I'm sorry I broke your coffee cup – it was an accident.

3

2 a 3 e 4 d 5 b 6 c

Unit 12

12A

1

a Across: 5 camel 6 bee 7 parrot; Down: 1 spider 2 gorilla 4 whale 8 tiger

2

a 2 had, finished 3 had worked 4 had got up 5 had, begun 6 had stolen
7 had missed 8 had stopped

b 2 began 3 left 4 was 5 had crashed 6 was 7 reached 8 had missed
9 had taken 10 arrived 11 tried 12 had sold 13 bought 14 spent
15 landed 16 didn't collect 17 had been 18 found 19 had closed
20 went

3

a Sound 1: come, done, run, won
Sound 2: fallen, taught
Sound 3: known, spoken, woke

12B

1

a 2 said, she would, me
3 told me, her, was watching, her
4 said, they'd been, their
5 told him, his, couldn't, them
6 told us, thought, they would go, their
7 said, she'd already done, her
8 told us, his, wasn't going to, his

b 2 He told me he would invite us to his house for dinner next week. / He told me that he would invite us to his house for dinner next week.
3 She told James he could use her computer to do his homework. / She told James that he could use her computer to do his homework.
4 He said the traffic had been really bad, so they had missed the 5:15 train. / He said that the traffic had been really bad, so they had missed the 5:15 train.
5 She told me they were going to buy me a lovely present for my birthday. / She told me that they were going to buy me a lovely present for my birthday.
6 He said he had tried calling his friend, but she hadn't answered, so he thought she was away on holiday. / He said that he had tried calling his friend, but she hadn't answered, so he thought she was away on holiday.

2

a Across: 5 sociable 7 serious 8 shy 10 anxious
Down: 1 careless 3 selfish 4 generous 6 creative 9 funny

12C

1

a 2 d 3 e 4 c 5 a 6 b 7 h 8 f

c 2 **B** You're absolutely right. 3 **B** Definitely. 4 **B** Oh, please.
5 **B** That's true. 6 **B** You're right.

2

a 2 Italian 3 British 4 San Francisco 5 Barcelona 6 American football

12D

1

a d

b True: 2, 4; False: 1, 3, 5

2

a 2 Later that day 3 The following morning 4 By morning
5 A few hours later

3

a **Possible answer:**
Last year, I went on a climbing trip in Scotland with three of my friends. We had only been there for a day when the accident happened. We had just got to the top of a mountain and we were eating some sandwiches that we'd made for lunch. Suddenly, the weather changed completely. It had been a clear, sunny day when we left the village where we were staying. However, now it was snowing heavily, and you could only see clearly for about 20 metres. We started walking down the path toward the next village where we were going to spend the night. The snow was getting deeper, so we walked slowly down the mountain. All of us were confident climbers, so we didn't think we would have any problems. Suddenly, I heard a shout from behind me. When I turned around my friend Anthony was lying on the ground. He said that he had fallen over a rock. As soon as I saw him, I knew it was serious. He said his leg was hurting badly and that he thought he had broken it. We decided to call for help. Fortunately, my phone had a signal, so I managed to call the emergency services.

After a while, the mountain rescue team arrived in their helicopter. They landed very close to where we were. They carried Anthony to the helicopter, and we all got in with him. Ten minutes later, we arrived at the hospital. Luckily, Anthony's leg wasn't badly broken, and they didn't need to operate. By the following day, Anthony was able to leave the hospital. We all felt very relieved.

David

Reading and listening extension

1

a 4, 1, 5, 2, 6, 3

b 2 anxious, was worried about changing something
3 generous, gave a lot of money to buy something
4 sociable, friendly with people

c 2 a 3 b 4 c

2

a 6, 5, 1, 8, 4, 7, 2, 3

b 2 a 3 b 4 b 5 a 6 b

Review and extension

1

2 I told her that she couldn't go to the beach by herself. / I told her she couldn't go to the beach by herself. / I said that she couldn't go to the beach by herself. / I said she couldn't go to the beach by herself.
3 He told me that my mother had called earlier that day. / He told me my mother had called earlier that day. / He said that my mother had called earlier that day. / He said my mother had called earlier that day.
4 We told her that her father wouldn't buy her a new computer. / We told her her father wouldn't buy her a new computer. / We said that her father wouldn't buy her a new computer. / We said her father wouldn't buy her a new computer.
5 Tom had never ridden a camel before, so he was quite nervous.
6 Our train had already left when we finally arrived at the station.

2

2 She's a really honest person. If shop assistants give her too much change, she always tells them.
3 He's very easygoing. I'm sure he won't mind if you bring your friend with you when you go to his house for dinner.
4 I'm not a very confident person. For example, I don't like speaking when I'm in a meeting with a large group of people.
5 Teachers have to learn to be patient with their students because sometimes they don't learn things immediately.
6 Why are you always so careless? You've already lost your phone twice this year!

3

2 At your age 3 old age 4 apart in age 5 at an early age
6 about my age

Vox pop video

Unit 1

a 2 through cycling 3 through friends
4 at language classes or dance classes 5 on trains or buses

b 2 c 3 d 4 a

c 2 a 3 b 4 a 5 c 6 a

Unit 2

a 2 b 3 b 4 a

b 2 b 3 c 4 a

c 2 c 3 a 4 b

Unit 3

a 2 Darren 3 Carolyn 4 Colin

b 2 six months ago 3 doesn't usually buy

c 2 c 3 b 4 a

Unit 4

a 2 b 3 c 4 a

b 2 meal with her friends 3 barbecue with her family 4 doesn't celebrate

c 2 c 3 d 4 a

Unit 5

a 2 b 3 c 4 a

b 2 talking to 3 friendly 4 science

c 2 c 3 d 4 a

Unit 6

a 2 c 3 a 4 b

b 2 Maibritt 3 Colin 4 Mark

c 2 b 3 a 4 c

Unit 7

a 2 a 3 b

b 1 Laurence 2 Darren 3 Peter

c 1 c 2 c 3 b

Unit 8

a 2 b 3 a

b 2 d 3 b 4 a

c 2 c 3 b 4 a

Unit 9

a 2 a 3 d 4 b

b 2 c 3 b 4 b

c 2 Carolyn 3 Matt 4 Lauren

Unit 10

a 2 b 3 b 4 c

b 2 c 3 b 4 b 5 a

c 2 would change seats 3 after five minutes 4 the people themselves
5 people that were making the noise

Unit 11

a 1 Dee Dee 2 Petros 3 James

b 2 d 3 a 4 b

c 2 b 3 a 4 c

Unit 12

a 2 d 3 b 4 e 5 a

b 2 b 3 a 4 c

c 2 b 3 a 4 b 5 a